Doctor
Whom

Doctor Whom

or

ET Shoots and Leaves

The Zero Tolerance
Approach to Parodication

A R R R ROBERTS

The right of A. R. R. Roberts to be identified as the
author of this work has been asserted by him in accordance
with the Copyright, Designs and Patents Act 1988.

First published in Great Britain in 2006 by
Gollancz
An imprint of the Orion Publishing Group
Orion House, 5 Upper St Martin's Lane,
London WC2H 9EA

This edition published in Great Britain
in 2007 by Gollancz

1 3 5 7 9 10 8 6 4 2

A CIP catalogue record for this book
is available from the British Library

ISBN 13 978 0 57507 968 7
ISBN 10 0 57507 968 1

Typeset by Input Data Services Ltd, Frome

Printed in Great Britain at Mackays of Chatham plc,
Chatham, Kent

The Orion Publishing Group's policy is to use papers that
are natural, renewable and recyclable products and made
from wood grown in sustainable forests. The logging and
manufacturing processes are expected to conform to the
environmental regulations of the country of origin.

www.orionbooks.co.uk

PREAMBLE

The extraterrestrial pointed his oddly-shaped weapon at the Dr. 'This is the end,' he said. 'This is goodbye *forever*, Doctor! No longer shall your kind oppress the Galaxy with your terrible grammatical correctitude—'

'—ness,' corrected the Dr, in a small voice. Even though he had his arms up, and a gun pressed against his chest, he couldn't help it.

'You *die* now!' screeched the infuriated ET.

'Don't be so sure!' said the Dr, defiantly. 'You'll find I'm harder to kill than you might assume ...'

'Not *this* time, Doctor. Do you see what I'm holding in my hand? It's a TGV. *Oh* yes.'

'No!' gasped the Dr, his face paling. By which I mean, becoming more like a paling. You know: thinning, and acquiring the metallic sheen of terror. 'A Time Gentleman Violator? But those weapons are *outlawed* by the convention of —'

'Outlawed, yes,' agreed the ET. 'Despised and condemned by all civilised people in the Galaxy. And why? Because they are *deadly* to Time Gentlemen! The *only* weapon that bypasses your infuriating ability to *re-un-degenerate yourselves* at the moment of death!' The ET laughed. It would be a cliché to say he laughed maniacally. A cliché, but nevertheless true. He laughed like a maniac; a little green spacealien maniac. His laughter was mainy. Maniac-like. Manicalesque. Then he spoke:

'Oh the adventures I had! The money I have spent! The crosses I have doubled! And all to obtain this little weapon – and to arrange matters such that I could be here, now, able to point it at you, Doctor, and pull – this – trigger.'

'I still don't see,' said the Dr, 'how you were able to trace me *here*?'

'You don't see?' said the ET. 'Why, you have a traitor aboard your TARDY, dear Doctor! One of your companions has betrayed you!'

'No!' the Dr gasped, spinning about to stare at the two of us. 'One of you two? But I trusted you! I showed you the galaxy! And you *betrayed* me ...?'

We were too shocked to reply.

'Only *one* of them betrayed you, Doctor,' said the ET. 'Now I could tell you which one ... but, you know what? I think I prefer to kill you *without* letting you know! I *like* the idea of you going to your ultimate death with that little irritant nagging in your brain.'

'Wait–' the Dr cried, starting forward, his hands raised before him. 'You mustn't– you couldn't– you daren't–'

The ET pressed the muzzle of his weapon close up against the Dr's chest, so as to be quite sure there was no chance of the shot going wide.

He pulled the trigger and the hideous weapon discharged. Its explosive bolt of time-energy crashed catastrophically into the Dr's torso.

'You dared!' the Dr gasped, staggered back. 'You could!'

'I *musted*,' said the ET, triumphfully. 'I *did must*.'

'I'm dying,' the Dr rasped. 'Quick ... loosen my tie ...'

'No!' cried Linn, rushing to the supine form of the Dr. 'It cannot be!'

'It can, it are,' said the ET. 'And now, after I am shot you in the body, I shall be off. The blow has been struck! We can stick our temporal apostrophes – or indeed, apostrophe's – where-ever the Punc we like! The tyranny of grammar is at an end! *I* is leaving.' And so the ET, having fatally injured the Dr, walked back to his unconventionally shaped time-and-space ship, stepped inside and closed the door behind itself. A moment later the craft shimmered and faded from existence.

And we were stranded with a dead Dr.

Behind us, in the recesses of the room, strange monstrous forms of life writhed and seethed in their green-lit tanks.

Well.

Or maybe it didn't happen *quite* like that. But I think I've captured the gist of it.

Oh, I'm sorry? Did you want *more* than the gist?

CONTENTS

Chapter Twelve

THE END

'Well,' said the Dr, standing at the control panel. 'Everything seems to have worked out alright in the end. Again!'

I snuggled into the arms of my new love; and she snuggled into mine. Not to put too fine a point on it, we snuggled into one another's arms. It was snug. 'I never thought I'd see this day, Doctor,' I said. 'I truly believed that my happiness boat had sailed. That my happiness rocket had blasted off into orbit without me in the cockpit. That the happiness tortoise has crawled off just out of my reach.'

'Can I drop you two lovebirds anywhere?' the Dr asked. 'It's on my way.'

'How do you know it's on your way,' my beautiful partner asked, from the cradle of my arms, 'if you don't know where we want to go?'

'Everywhere's on my way,' said the Dr. 'That's the beauty of a craft like the TARDY.'

'It almost feels,' I said, 'too good to be true! It's almost as if it's too good for me to believe it.'

'Tush,' said the Dr. 'Don't say that.'

Oh it seemed like the happiest of happy endings! But in my heart, inside that heart, in the heart inside my heart, I knew that it wasn't. I knew that it was something the reverse. 'There's the outstanding matter of the hydrogen atom . . .' I said, prompted by my nagging conscience.

'The hydrogen atom,' repeated the Dr nodding sagely.

'*The* hydrogen atom?' asked my love. 'Singular case?'

'Yes. There's only one, apparently,' I said.

'Well, we'll cross that bridge when we get to it,' said the Dr. 'Don't worry about it. As we stand, we've ridden the cosmos of an unspeakable evil. We've sorted out your love life. We've averted what seemed like inevitable destruction. I think we can afford to cut ourselves a little slack.'

'Take us to the star Thpops,' I said; 'and the world Tapov, where the dancing never ends. Take us both there so that we can get on with the rest of our lives!'

The Dr touched the panel. 'With the greatest of pleasure.'

And so we hurtled through time and space. But like I said; appearances can be deceptive, and a happy ending need not, perhaps, be so happy as all that.

Chapter Two

THE DIMENSIONS OF THE TARDY

The TARDY is bigger on the inside than on the out. That is, of course, the fact that anybody who has seen the Dr's craft remembers about it. But few people think through the implications of this state of affairs.

For example: toilets. The smallest room in a TARDY is actually, of course, the *biggest* room. Going to the loo involves sitting on a porcelain pan in the middle of an empty aircraft hangar. Breezes moan and whisper in the rafters. The toilet paper chitters and flaps in the holder at your side. It is intensely cold.

Very hard to concentrate on the job in hand, I can tell you.

The converse is also true. The engine-room of the TARDY contains Matter-Dolorosa Spacetime Converter Generators, vast machines that wrench the very sub-material of space and time about itself, plaiting great ropes of superstring into cat's-cradles shapes. These are the largest and most powerful motors in the cosmos.

The engine room is the size and shape of a small cigar box.

The TARDY was designed with enormous cargo-holds, such that the Dr could transport millions of metric tonnes of cargo from world to world, should he need so to do. But, although the design was faithfully followed the fact remains that, stepping through the door of the device, you discover that the cargo holds on the inside are the exact size and dimensions of the ashtray on the Ford Cortina Mark III.

The control room presented a similar dilemma. It was designed to be spacious, with a large viewscreen and many padded and swivelly chairs, arranged carefully on a split-level effect, with various complicated-looking consoles and podiums between them. But when he took possession of his craft the Dr discovered that the bridge was the size of a glove-compartment. Luckily the design for the bridge had also included a glove compartment, which (stepping inside the TARDY) turned out to be the size of a middle-sized TV studio. The Dr had cleared it out: throwing away the half-eaten packet of Werther's Originals, the single left-hand glove, a one-inch-to-a-light-year galactic road atlas with the cover missing and the page for 'Earth's solar system' all creased and scuffy, the half a dozen paperclips and the old biro with the ink clotted at the wrong end. He had then been able to re-route the control surfaces to a panel in the new room. He took to calling this space 'the bridge', but it was really the glove-compartment.

But this peculiar disrelation between inside and outside was not the only strange feature of the TARDY.

One feature of the machine was that it possessed a capability to disguise itself automatically. Unfortunately this 'Disguise Mutation Chip' functioned perfectly. This was a terrible shame. It would have been much better had it broken down, or malfunctioned in some way. But we had no such luck.

You see, the Dr's TARDY took the shape of a police phone box. That was its disguise, which enabled it to blend in on any world. All Time Gentlemen were given TARDIES, and all of them were configured with some sort of police-based disguise chip, because every civilisation in the galaxy has a police force. But I have to say, if I'd been the Dr, taking charge of my TARDY for the first time, I would have flipped open the panel in the central control module and I would have smashed the Disguise Mutation Chip with the heel of my fancy boot. Or with a hammer. Or the head of my nearest assistant. Anything to hand.

Do you ask why? I'll tell you why.

The Disguise Mutation Chip automatically changed the outward appearance of the TARDY to blend in with its environment. Imagine a different TARDY, one operated by a notional Time Gentleman, and programmed to look like a police car. It might land in London in the 1960s as a panda car; and in London in the 2960s as a Police All Nodes Driving AcceleraTron. Blending-in, you see.

All well and good – *if* your TARDY is configured to look like a police car. Or a police station. But the Dr's TARDY took the shape of a police *phone box*. It was a nightmare.

Oh, if we landed in the London of the late 1950s then things were fine. We would materialise ourselves on the corner of a foggy street looking exactly like a tall blue cubicle with POLICE at the top. Well and dandy. But let's say we were happened to materialise in London in – let's say, for the sake of argument – 2010. Nobody used *phone boxes* in that time-period any more, of course; mobile phone technology had rendered them obsolete. To blend in, the TARDY's software would automatically give us the appearance of a small Nokia seven-three-fourteen, the one with the blue screen and caller ident, the size of a small pack of cards.

Have you ever tried to clamber *out* of a small mobile phone? Of course you haven't. That's a stupid question. Well, I have: and let me tell you: even with the flip-back top it is very far from being easy.

Once the Dr landed the TARDY on a planet in the Nibbler Nebula, a place where the local inhabitants had not advanced beyond the equivalent of our stone age. Their rudimentary police force communicated amongst itself by yelling. Accordingly our Disguise Mutation Chip manifested us as a six-foot shouty man. We had to climb out through his mouth – awkward. And messy too. I came out first, squeezing myself up the gullet and past the big rubbery tongue and slobbery lips: I fell six feet to the stony soil, bruising my shoulder. I picked myself up and did my best to wipe the saliva from my face and body, as Linn followed, and finally the Dr himself. After a great deal of effort, and a good deal of saying *yuk* and *euw* we were all outside, and about to leave, when the Dr cursed. 'I have forgotten my Moronic Screwdriver! Left it inside the TARDY!'

Linn and I both stared at one another. For several minutes nothing happened, except for the moaning of a vast and distant wind dragging itself across the horizon-spanning stony desert.

'Well,' I prompted. 'Do you want to pop back inside and get it?'

The Dr looked at the TARDY. Its Disguise Mutation Chip had given it the look of a man not unlike a young Brian Blessed. The door was still open. The Dr looked at me. 'You don't fancy just, er, *popping* back inside for me, do you?'

'Not I,' I said.

'Well,' said the Dr, putting his hand on the TARDY's chin and snapping it upwards to shut the door. 'I don't suppose we'll need it.'

And so we went off without the Moronic Screwdriver. It was alright in the end, because we didn't need it; but you take my point. It's not convenient.

On another occasion we landed in eighteenth-century England, and the TARDY took the form of a large sema-phore flag: oak pole and a red-triangular pennant. On the distant World of Racrd it took the form of a carrier pigeon. On more than one occasion (I repeat, for the record: on *more* than one occasion) we landed in cultures so technologically sophisticated that police com-munication was affected by microscopic nano-tech-nological prostheses. On these occasions the Dr would open the TARDY door from the inside just fine; but the attempt to step through, or even to put one's little finger through, proved perfectly impossible.

'Righty-tighty,' the Dr would say, on these occasions. 'Well, I didn't really want to visit this world and this timeframe anyway.' And he'd fiddle with the control knobs and away we'd go.

There were whole swathes of space and time we never visited.

Chapter One

THE INTERVIEW

The Dr (the advertisement said) happened to be in my area and was recruiting. I went through his usual channels, and was given a time for my interview.

This took place in a spaceship, a marvellous device. It was called the TARDY, because its temporal engines slip it out of synch with Standard Time, disengaging itself, becoming in a sense cosmically *delayed*. It flips back along the temporal dimension (if the destination is in the future, then the TARDY loops right the way round the whole of spacetime, over the top and back in. It takes less time than you might think).

I stepped through the door. The Dr and a young woman were sitting behind a table. It was one of those tables with fold-out metal tubing for legs.

The Dr was dressed in a strange collection of velvet jacket, moleskin trousers, black winklepinker boots, a waistcoat, a silk tie with the design of a rectangular blue grid upon it. He had a big woolly scarf, and was wearing a leather overjacket. He looked a power of odd, to be honest. The young lady was dressed more soberly. And attractively.

'Hello,' said the Dr, peering at his notes and not looking at me. 'Please take a seat.' There was a rather rickety-looking chair sitting in the middle of the room:

four aluminium poles, a small square of red plastic upholstery and a scuffed oval-shaped seat. I sat on this gingerly.

The woman smiled at me, which I took to be an encouraging sign. The Dr, however, seemed to be spending an awfully long time going through my résumé.

'Right,' he said, eventually. Finally he looked up and met my eye. 'I am the Dr and this is Linnaeus Trout. Named for the great Linnaeus, who did such sterling work establishing categories, rules and restrictive definitions.'

This meant nothing to me. 'Right,' I said, a little nervously.

'Hello,' she said.

'Good afternoon,' I said.

'So— Mr— *Tailor*, is it?'

'That's right. Prose Tailor.'

'I wasn't sure,' the Dr said, 'if that was your name, or your job description?'

'It's both,' I explained. 'On my world it is our jobs that give us our names.'

'I see. So if, let us say, your work were syringing out the build-up of wax from the ears of cataleptic pigs, then your name would be—?'

'Please forgive the Doctor his levity,' said the woman, speaking in a well-modulated and pleasant voice. 'Why don't we start the interview with you telling us why you want the job?'

'I don't know really,' I said, rubbing my right knee with my right hand. 'I suppose I'm ready for a change. A career change. I've been a Prose Tailor now for seven years, and I've got the feeling I'm going nowhere. I'm ready for the change and the, um, exciting challenges of a new position.'

I paused. I don't mind admitting I was nervous. I've never handled job interviews very well. I rubbed my right knee with my right hand again. Then I rubbed my left knee with my left hand for a bit. Then (I'm not sure why, except that I was terribly nervous) I rubbed both my knees with both my hands simultaneously. This produced a slightly squeaky noise, and for some reason I rubbed both my knees again, replicating the squeaky noise and satisfying myself that it had not been some random noise that happened to coincide with my knee-rubbing activity. I looked up. The two people behind the desk were looking at me askance. Or if not exactly quite *askance*, then at least in a way that was far from being fully skance. This, naturally, made me more nervous.

I folded my arms. But then I thought that folded arms might give me a standoffish look, so I unfolded them again. I found myself wishing that I had a desk, like my interviewers, upon which to rest my arms in a casual and easygoing manner. I held my arms, elbows bent, a little away from my sides. But that was no good.

'Mr Tailor,' said the Dr, leaning forward a little. 'This is a job that will involve a great deal of travelling through space and time. Tell me: what experience of time travel will you bring to the position?'

I decided then that the best thing to do was let my arms hang straight down by my sides. But no sooner had I let them droop than it occurred to me that this might look rather monkey-like. I didn't want them to think me too simian. Why should they give the job to a simian? So I picked my arms up and lay them in my lap. This was better, except that it meant that my hands were resting in the declivity of my crotch. As soon as I had made this move I regretted it. I didn't want them to think, after all, that I was some kind of pervert, fondling myself in the crotch-area right in the middle of an interview. If they wouldn't want to give the job to a simian, how much less would they want to give it to a crotch-fondler? So, and trying to be as discreet as I could, I turned both of my hands over, so that instead of resting palms down on my groin they were resting palms *upward* on my thighs. This went well, except that somehow the very tip of my right thumb got itself snagged under a fold of cloth in my trousers, such that as I moved it away the thumb *drew up* a sort of mini-tent of fabric from the material loosely folded in at my crotch. When I finished this little man-oeuvre with my hands this upraised pyramid of cloth remained standing. I glanced down. This could not be making a good impression. It looked, in fact, as if I were markedly and inappropriately aroused by the mere fact of being interviewed for a job. Drastic action was required. With sudden and explosive action I coughed, shifted in my seat, and slapped my right hand down to my privates to smooth away this upward-poking fold of trouser cloth. Then, to try and cover the operation, I swung my right leg up and over my left.

That, I told myself, was one smooth manoeuvre.

My two interviewers were staring at me. The woman had her mouth slightly open.

'I'm sorry,' I said. 'What was the question again?'

'I was asking you,' the Dr repeated, in a wary voice, 'what experience of time travel you would bring to the position.'

'Ah. Well, just the usual, I suppose. The standard?'

'The standard experience?'

'Yes, you know. One hour per hour, travelling through time, that sort of thing.'

'Travelling forward?'

'Yes.'

'Your résumé,' the Dr pointed out, placing his forefinger on the relevant bit, 'suggests that you have experience of travelling backwards in time as well.'

'Yes,' I said. 'Well, in a manner of speaking.'

'A manner of speaking?'

'Yes. It was last year. A haircut.'

'Haircut?'

'It made me three or four years younger. Everybody said so. At *least* three years and possibly four.'

'It *made you* three or four years younger,' Linn asked, 'or it made you *look* three or four years younger?'

'Yes,' I said. 'One of those two.'

'Mr Tailor,' said the Dr, sharply. 'Do you understand what the job particulars involve?'

'I think so, yes.'

'It is more than simply *travelling*. We have a series of very important missions to accomplish, repairing and indeed correcting the very *nature* of spacetime.'

'I understand.'

'There is sometimes danger. Are you prepared for danger?'

'Danger is my middle name.'

The Dr frowned, and picked up a pen. 'You really should have put that down,' he said, making the correction.

'No,' I said. 'It's not literally my middle name. That's just a way of saying that, yes, I'm prepared for danger.'

The Dr, frowning in a more pronounced fashion, scribbled out what he had just written.

'Mr Tailor,' put in Linn. 'Let me tell you what it was about your application that interested us. You are a prose tailor?'

'I am.'

'You tailor prose?'

'Yes.'

'Clearly you are familiar with punctuation. Grammar. Correct syntax. That's *very* important.'

'Well,' I said. 'Yes I am.'

'Allow me to explain,' said the Dr. 'This is more than a matter of prose. You see time, history, the life of the cosmos – it has a grammar. There are *rules*. When actual existence violates those rules, somebody needs to step in and *do something*. Somebody needs to go around correcting the *solecisms* and *ambiguities* that creep in. Because, if nobody did that ...' He trailed off.

'What?'

'It would be too ghastly to contemplate,' he said, firmly. 'Wouldn't it, Linn?'

'Much too ghastly,' she agreed.

'I see,' I said in an obviously *I've no idea what you're talking about* tone of voice.

'You need to think of history as a kind of sentence,' said the Dr. 'Take your own history: the history of the

Planet of the Asexual Slug-men. Now, in the *third* quarter of the—'

'Earth,' said Linn.

'What?'

'We decided to go to Earth instead,' said Linn. 'Don't you remember?'

'We're on Earth?' the Dr asked. 'And *not* the Planet of the Asexual Slug-men?'

'That's right,' Linn said.

The Dr looked me up and down. There was a pause. 'You sure?' he said.

'Earth *is* my planet,' I said, a little nervously.

'Well if you say so, if you, yes. Start again. Take *your* own history, Mr Tailor: the history of the Planet *Earth*, apparently. Take a figure like Leonardo da Vinci. It's pretty obvious, I think, that da Vinci was born too *early* in your planet's history. Do you see? He started having all these ideas that were well before their time. You see, Earth's history was *building up* to Leonardo.'

'He was born ahead of his time,' I said.

'Yes. You could say that.'

'And it's wrong for people to be ahead of their time?'

'Not *morally* wrong,' the Dr clarified. '*Grammatically* wrong. Those are two different usages of the word *wrong*, you understand. Take that sentence, the one I spoke a moment ago: *Earth's history was building up to Leonardo.* If Leonardo occurs too early in that sentence it makes nonsense of it:

Earth's Leonardo history was building up to.

That's a very unsatisfying sentence. You see that, don't you?'

'In fact,' Linn put in, 'the situation is even more pronounced than that. You see, the sentence of Time is structured according to the *logic* of sequential time. Time is one thing *after* another, isn't it? That's what chronology *means*. Because of that, Leonardo's too-early appearance actually disrupts everything that follows. It warps the sentence into something more like this:

Earth's Leonardo buildtoing up history was.

And that's an even *more* unsatisfying sentence.'

'So,' I said, realization dawning, 'your job is—'

'To buzz about the cosmos, making the necessary corrections. Affirming the grammar of Time. Adding an apostrophe here, changing a *who* to a *whom* there, as it were. Changing history in little ways to keep the overall story – the cosmic *hi*story – flowing properly on according to the rules.'

'So you're going to sort out Leonardo, are you?'

'Going to? I did him last year. In the original timeline he was Aviator King of a United Europe from fourteen-ninety-one to sixteen-sixty-six.'

'That's an awfully long time to be king,' I observed.

'Yes. He discovered an anti-aging potion. He called it Gniga. That's "aging" backwards. Because it was anti-aging. Do you see?'

'So you put an end to that possible time sentence?' I said.

'We corrected it, yes.'

'How?'

'We photocopied all his notebooks backwards and then snaffled the originals. Puzzled him no *end*, I don't mind telling you. Took him *years* to figure them out. Anyway, that's off the point. The *point* is that we need somebody who understands grammar – who understands the rules – to assist us in our work. I am a fully qualified Time Gentleman. Linn, here, is my apprentice; after seven years she will be eligible to take the Time Gentleman exams. Are you ready to join our exciting and dynamic team?'

'I think so,' I said.

'You *think* so?' prompted Linn. 'Or you *know* so?'

'I *know* so.'

'You *think* you know so?' asked the Dr. 'Or you *know* you know so?'

'I know I know so!' I said, assertively. 'And, just to be clear, I know I know I know so, and I know I know I know I know so.'

'Good. Well Mr Tailor,' the Dr was shuffling his papers, 'that's all the questions we wanted to ask you, I think. Do you have any questions you want to ask *us*?'

'Well,' I said. 'I was wondering about overtime?'

The Dr looked at Linn, and Linn looked at the Dr. Then, for reasons mysterious to me, they both started laughing. 'Very good, Mr Tailor!' the Dr said. 'Very witty. We like you. Welcome aboard.'

'Witty?' I asked, nervously.

And so began my adventures with the Dr.

Chapter Four

THE DOOM OF THE *ICETANIC*

The TARDY rematerialised inside a large white space: bare and spare and perfectly white. 'We're here,' declared the Dr.

'And where's here, exactly?' Linn asked him.

'Earth. But the real question is *when*. Let's pop outside, have a peep.'

He opened the door and we all stepped outside.

The TARDY had taken the form of a large rectangular blue box with the word POLICE written at the top of all four of its faces. 'Well,' said the Dr, rubbing his chin in an *Antiques Roadshow* sort of way. 'I'd say, looking at the design, we're talking somewhere around nineteen-ten. Which is pretty good, considering I was aiming at London in the eighteen-eighties. Not *too* far from the target, now, is it.'

'We're thirty years too late!' I objected.

'No such thing as late,' said the Dr, blithely. 'You know what they say. Wherever you find yourself, there you are. I daresay there's a kink or temporal solecism for us to work out hereabouts. Put our time-grammatical knowledge to good use.'

'Caves,' said Linn, looking around her. 'It's *extremely* cold.'

'Far as I can tell, these walls,' I offered, running my

ungloved finger along one of them, 'are *ice*.'

'Ice, you say?' said the Dr coming over to check for himself. 'You could be right Prosy. Ice, ice, maybe.'

'So we're inside an ice-cave somewhere on Earth in nineteen-ten,' said Linn, matter of factly. 'Could it be the north pole?'

'Or the south?' I suggested.

'Or the west,' agreed the Dr. 'One of those, definitely.'

'West pole?' I said. 'There's no west pole.'

'Indeed there is,' said the Dr. 'Very cold it is too.'

'And where is it, then?'

'Oh, not to worry. I mean, it's in Wales. But not to worry. I was hoping to show you London in the eighteen-eighties. I need to get hold of this chap from the East End ... somebody from your time period, Tailor.'

'From Earth's twenty-third century?' I asked. 'Really?'

'Indeed. Fellow called Jack. A much misunderstood individual; he was suspected of a number of rather nasty crimes —'

'You're not talking about Jack the Ripper?' asked Linn, in horror.

'Jack the *Rapper*,' corrected the Dr. 'As I say, he was a Rhyme-tailor from the twenty-third century – from Prosy's time period in fact.'

'*Please* don't call me Prosy,' I said in a small voice.

'The twenty-third century,' the Dr continued. 'The time period when Earth was governed by the world state of You-Say! and everybody was encouraged to express themselves through the medium of tuneless shouting. A low point in Earth's history, I'd say. Anyway my friend

Jack got dislodged in time and after a series of bizarre adventures, into which I really don't have time, right now, to go, he migrated to the East End of London in the eighteen-eighties. He's there now. He likes it there, although his habit of shouting rhyming couplets at people in street has been misconstrued. He's out of his place; as naked a temporal solecism as you can imagine.'

'He gets naked?'

'No *he's* not naked. The solecism is naked. By which I mean, egregious. Obvious. And my job is to sort that out – recover him and return him to his own time. Set the time-line straight again.'

'Are you going to do this *before* or *after* he murders all those prostitutes?' Linn demanded.

'Before, obviously. That way I prevent all the suffering he creates. Everybody wins. He's not a bad sort, either, by all accounts. It's just that his brain is a bit scrambled by the temporal dislocation. It almost always results in disaster, does temporary dislocation. I should imagine Mr Prose here would welcome the chance of a bit of chinwag with a contemporary, eh?'

'Frankly,' I said. 'I have enough trouble with Rhymetailors patronizing me as a poor humble tailor of prose at home, without wanting to meet another one on my travels. Beside. We're obviously *not* in east London.'

'It's so *cold*,' said Linn. 'Can we just get back inside the TARDY before I freeze to death?'

'No no,' the Dr expostulated. 'Let's have a little look around, shall we?' And with that he marched off.

*

We left the ice cave through an opening at the back and

passed into a long ice-corridor. This split into two, one sloping downwards to the left and one rising to the right. 'This seems,' the Dr was saying, 'to be a natural cave formation. We should go *right*, here, I think.'

We all trudged up the slope.

'So is this the north or the south pole?' Linn asked.

'I've come to a conclusion. This ice is dry – it's very cold. I believe we're in an Antarctic cave-system, formed by natural forces. Now, in nineteen-ten the Antarctic continent was completely unexplored. Right now we're perhaps three thousand miles from the nearest human being.'

'I say!' cried a human being, perhaps three metres away from us. 'Are you chaps English? Or do my ears deceive me?'

He was a young man dressed in a smart, Edwardian-era military uniform: olive-green heavy fabric and military greatcoat. The outfit was topped-off with a hat. Not a top hat, I should add, in case my use of the phrase *topped-off with a hat* gives that impression. That would be silly, under the circumstances. It was a *fur* hat, with ear flaps like two great furry tongues hanging down on each side of his face. Fur, you see, is a better head-insulator than is, er, top. Than whatever top-hats are made of. Anyway this fellow also wore Eskimo-mittens, and snowboots: he was evidently a military officer clearly prepared for the cold.

'Good afternoon,' said the Dr, brightly.

'Afternoon? But it's the middle of the night!'

'Really? It's awfully bright.'

'Of course it's bright in *here*,' said the man. 'The

corridors are illuminated. With electricity, you know.'
A certain pride was audible in his voice as he said this
last thing. 'There's a mirror system beaming light down
all the ... but, wait a mo, you haven't answered my
question.'

'Question?'

'Are you English?'

'I am,' I said. 'My name is Prose Tailor. And this is
Linn.'

'How do you do?' asked Linn.

'And this,' I concluded, 'is the Doctor.'

'Pleased to meet you,' drawled the fellow. 'My name
is Captain Antenealle.'

'Antenealle?' repeated Linn, with the very *slightest* of
disbelieving intonations.

'It's a perfectly common Wiltshire surname I assure
you,' said Antenealle, blushing slightly. Or perhaps it
was the cold.

'If I might *say* so,' said the Dr, 'you don't seem all that
surprised to see us all here, in Antarctica.'

'Were we in Antarctica,' said Antenealle, 'I might be.
Surprised, I mean.'

'So we're *not* in Antarctica?' said Linn.

'We are not.'

'In which case,' she pressed, 'where *are* we?'

'Where else but aboard a secret Habakkuk-style
British Navy Warship in the middle of the North Atlantic
in the winter of nineteen-twelve?'

'I knew it!' cried the Dr, eurekaishly.

Both Linn and I looked at him. 'You knew what?'

'The North Atlantic. I *knew* that's where we were!'

'Well, no you didn't,' pointed out Linn. 'You said we were in Antarctica.'

The Dr looked pained. 'Atlantic—*a*,' he said, after a short pause. 'Is what I said—*Atlantica*, which is as everybody knows, or at least everybody *should* know, is the official Latin name of the, um.' He paused for a moment, then added 'of, Atlantica is, um.'

He seemed to dry up. He dropped his gaze to the floor for a while. Nobody said anything for long seconds.

'Anyway,' said Linn, turning back to Captain Antenealle. 'Whether we're in Antarctica, or aboard a secret HMS warship in the North Atlantic, either way I think I would expect to be just a *little* surprised to see us.'

'Well the truth is,' said the Captain, with a little chivalrous bow, 'that after all this strange business with the chanting knights in silver armour nothing surprises me any more.'

'Chanting knights?' repeated the Dr.

'In silver armour, yes.'

'Is that with a k?'

'Is the armour with a k? Wouldn't that be karmour?'

'The knights – are they ker-nights, or just nights?'

'The former. It's most peculiar. They seem to be overrunning us. We try our best to fight them off, but bullets don't seem to stop them – they're *ghosts* from the *crusades*, some of the men say. The men are simple Tommies, of course, not officer class. So whilst they're brave as lions in the face of physical danger, supernatural danger unnerves them. *They* say we should all abandon ship.'

'Ghosts from the crusades, you say?'

'That's what the men think.'

'And you don't agree?'

'Not in the least,' said the Captain, matter-of-factly. 'I ask myself: why should ghosts from the crusades come dressed up in shiny silver armour to visit a secret Navy ship sculpted from a solid block of ice sailing in the North Atlantic in nineteen-twelve, whilst war with the Germans seems imminent?'

'You're awfully free with your secret information,' I observed.

'But you're English,' said Antenealle, in a *there you go!* sort of voice.

'Nineteen-twelve,' said the Dr. 'Seems to me that date should be familiar to me. Nineteen-twelve, nineteen-twelve, can't think why.'

'You lot had better come with me,' said the Captain Antenealle. 'See if we can't scrounge a cup of tea. If there's one problem with these Habakkuk craft it's keeping the tea nice and hot.'

*

We fell into step behind this young military man, and marched up the corridor.

'Project Habakkuk,' said the Dr. 'I always thought it was just a rumour. But here we are, actually aboard one of their craft! Very exciting. Officially, of course, it never got off the drawing board.'

'You've *heard* of this Habakkuk Project?' Linn asked.

'Of course! It's famous. It was a British Naval plan to sculpt huge ships out of ice. The advantage of *ice* as a raw-material for shipbuilding is that it is quite unsinkable. Unlike the iron out of which, say, dread-noughts are built. Iron – and I don't know if you've ever noticed this – but iron *sinks*. Sinks pretty comprehensively, really. Down it goes! But ice ... well, let me put it this way. If you've ever dunked a battleship-shaped chunk of ice-cream into a milkshake, you'll know that—'

'Are you *sure*?' I said. 'It sounds daft to me.'

'Nonsense. It was a brilliant idea; one of the few brilliant ideas the Royal Navy ever had. A very large ice battleship would be a superb weapon of naval warfare. The main drawback would be a *certain amount* of difficulty in manoeuvre; but on the plus side it would be near-enough impossible for enemy ships to sink the craft ... even if they knocked big chunks off it with artillery shells the remainder would still float along. I just hadn't realised that the Navy got as far as actually building a prototype ship.'

'Well we did,' said Antenealle over his shoulder. 'We built it, crewed it, and assigned it a complement of marines ... my men, in fact. We're on secret manoeuvres here right now. Things were going swimmingly until—'

'The ghosts from the crusades?'

'Well I'm a sceptic,' said Antenealle cheerily. 'For instance, one thing that makes me doubt the whole *ghost* theory is the way they bump into things. Slip over, crash into walls, that sort of thing.'

'Maybe they're slapstick ghosts?'

'Never heard of that sort. And the *other* thing worth mentioning is that they're *pretty* heavily armed. I never heard of ghosts going about carrying artillery. Some chains to rattle, maybe. But not, you know, rifles and hand-cannons. And woo-oo-*oo*! Wooooooo! That's what you'd expect, isn't it? An owl-like woo-ooing. Wooooooooooooooooo! But that's not the noise these chaps make *at all*.'

'What noise *do* they make?' asked Linn.

'It's a sort of oo-aah noise. Oo-aah. Very strange.'

✱

We finally came through into the carved-out ice-chamber that functioned as the ship's bridge. A man dressed as an able-seaman was at the big spokey wheel thing (I've temporarily forgotten the technical term for this piece of equipment; but you know the thing I mean; the wagon-wheel shaped thing that does the ship's steery-steery). Next to him was a man in a blue officer's uniform. Panels and consoles of teak inlaid with brightly polished brass were ranged around the space. An electrical light dangled from the low roof. Straight ahead there was a very narrow window, a slit no more than a couple of inches high, through which the sailor was looking. Outside the night was pitchy black.

'Ah, Captain!' declared the officer as we came onto the bridge. 'Good to see you again. And who are these?'

'A Doctor and his friends, Commodore Sthree-Tymsa-Lady,' said Antenealle. 'They're English, don't worry.'

'Splendid,' said Tymsa-Lady. 'Welcome to the HMS *Icetanic*! I say, would you three mind awfully *pitching in*, ma'am, gentlemen? We're having a touch of bother with these silver fellows. All hands would be *much* appreciated at the pumps, don't you know.'

'Glad to help,' said the Dr. 'That's an interesting

surname, by the way. Are you related to the Hampshire Tymsa-Ladies?'

'Different branch of the family,' said the Commodore brightly. 'My grandmother married Henry Sthree, one of the Middlesex Sthrees. They moved to Surrey. I didn't catch *your* name, I'm afraid?'

'I'm called Whom,' said the Dr.

'Now that *is* an interesting surname!' said the Commodore, clearly impressed. 'Very distinctive! And your friends?'

'This is Miss Trout. And this young man is Prose Tailor.'

The Commodore turned to face me. 'Any relation of Pinny Tailor?' he asked.

'Um,' I said.

The Commodore seemed to take this as a yes. 'Pinny Tailor! The old donkey! How is he? Still Secretary of State for Imperial Affairs?'

'I wonder, Commodore,' the Dr put in, 'if you could tell me a little about these ghosts supposedly haunting your secret ice-built Habakkuk-project ship. You see, I'm here on a ... um, government mission to undertake certain ... secret activities, for the secret services of ... you know. Government stuff.'

'Government mission?' repeated the Commodore.

'We were dropped onto the ship by, er, hot-air balloon,' said the Dr. 'That's how we've suddenly appeared, as if by the magic of matter-transference and rematerialisation, on your ship in the middle of the ocean, without any advance warning. I mean, obviously we *haven't* appeared by matter-transference. That would be silly. It's most definitely, you know. Balloons.'

'I assumed it would be something like that,' said the Commodore.

'Anyway, I was wondering about these apparitions. I've a suspicion that they might have a part to play in the ... mission of which I was speaking. Did you say they were *silver* men?'

'They've practically over-run the ship,' said the Commodore. 'The Captain has been down on the lower decks fighting them off. Haven't you, Antenealle? Down there with all your men?'

'They're all dead,' said the Captain. 'I'm sorry to say. Every last man-jack marine of them. Is there any tea? I'm parching for a cup.'

'*Oh* dear,' said the Commodore. '*All* of them?'

'Young Witherspoon was twitching a little when I left,' said Antenealle, filling a tin mug from a large brass urn. 'But I daresay he's a goner now. What with the size of the wound in his head. And also the three missing ....' The Captain paused to slurp his tea and go 'ahhh!,' before concluding, 'limbs.'

'*Oh* dear,' said the Commodore again. 'So, with all the able seamen gone too, that leaves ...?'

'Just us three,' said Antenealle. 'And, of course, our new friends.'

'Ah well,' said the Commodore. 'I suppose we'll just have to do our best.'

'They're all *dead*?' cried Linn in a horrified tone.

'Hmm' said the Captain.

'How can you be so extraordinarily blasé,' Linn demanded, 'in the face of such terrible loss of life?'

'Stiff upper lip,' said the Commodore. 'Or do I mean swift upper lip? I always get those confused.'

'Swift upper *cut*, I think it is, Commodore,' said Antenealle, taking another slurp of tea.

There was a distant explosion: muffled but unmistakeable. The ship shuddered. I could not contain a little yelp of terror.

'Don't worry ma'am,' said Antenealle, without looking at me. 'Those explosions might be worrying on a *regular* ship, but, you see, a Habakkuk-line vessel is literally unsinkable.'

'Oh the *Icetanic* is *quite* unsinkable,' agreed the Commodore. 'It's a miracle of modern design.'

'Perfectly unsinkable,' agreed the Captain. 'Can't be sunk.'

'No sinkee-sinkee,' declared the Commodore.

'Everything can happen *except* the kitchen sinking. By kitchen I mean the galley. And all the other parts of the ship too. None of them can sink.'

'So we've nothing to worry about then!' exclaimed the Dr, cheerfully.

'Well, there *is* one tiny little worry,' admitted the Commodore. 'My slight worry has to do with these silver men, the ones who've now slaughtered the entire crew and whom are now marching about shooting and blowing up everything in sight ... the worry is that they might be *German* agents, dressed up in some odd silver armour. They may be trying to seize the ship, to get hold of our military technology for the good of the Kaiser you see. We really can't allow that to happen. Our *problem*,' he went on, a little sorrowfully, 'is that I can't scuttle this ship. Normally of course I'd scuttle my ship to prevent her falling into enemy hands. But this ship is unscuttleabubble. I mean, of course, unscutable. Un,' he said, moving slowly through the syllables, 'Scut. Tle. A. Ble.'

'I see your dilemma,' said the Dr.

There was another explosion, somewhere below us. 'We'd better get down there,' said Antenealle, finishing his tea and plonking the mug back next to the brass urn. 'Come on!'

The Dr made as if to follow, but Linn grabbed his elbow. 'You're not going *after* him are you?' she hissed. 'Didn't you hear what happened to his men?'

'Of course,' the Dr hissed back. 'I feel certain that these strange silver men represent a pretty major grammatical error in the fabric of spacetime. Don't you? Do you really think that nineteen-twelve Earth should have creatures like that running around?'

'I suppose not,' said Linn, sulkily.

He walked smartly off the bridge; and, after exchanging a wary look, Linn and I followed.

*

The four of us went down some ice-carved staircases, and into a long corridor. The sound of explosions continued. These were not long-drawn out explosions, but short snappy blasts: not *bo-oo-oom*! Not even *boom*! *boom*!, but more like *bom*! *bom*!, or perhaps *bum-bum-bum*!

No. On second thoughts, that last one looks rather stupid, written down.

Anyway, let's just say that we could hear explosions. Interspersed amongst those percussive noises was the sound of gunfire, sharp and abrupt as the breaking of old bones: *rat, rat-tat, rat-tat*. Yes, that's good. That's exactly what the gunfire sounded like.

'We're definitely moving towards it,' said Linn, nervously. 'Those gunshots and explosions. They're getting louder.'

'I don't understand,' I said. 'If all your men are dead, Captain, what are these silver men shooting at?'

'Just at things in general I think,' said Antenealle. 'They don't seem too particular. They may just really enjoy shooting.'

The corridor opened into a wide ice cavern, a large groined space. Which is to say shaped (perhaps I should add for the sake of clarity) like a female rather than a male groin. Which, I mean, is what I've always assumed the phrase 'groined arches' to refer to. Unless I've got the wrong end of the stick there. That's very possible, you know.

'Ah,' said Antenealle. '*There* they are!' He sounded pleased. Pulling off one of his mittens and unbuttoning his holster, he drew his gun.

Directly in front of us was a rank of silvery, gleaming, robotic men. Nothing could be imagined that looked less like ghosts than these figures. They were the most solidly metallic and material fellows I ever saw. And what's more, they were marching slowly towards us.

'Tally ho!' said Antenealle. He levelled his pistol and fired three shots in quick succession. Then he started running directly towards the silvery men. There were pinging noises as his bullets ricocheted off their metallic chests.

One of these silver warriors lifted his hand, and a blast

of smoke and a blaze of noise slammed Antenealle off his feet. He landed on his back with a large, gooily tomato-coloured hole evident in his chest.

'Ooo,' said the Dr. 'That's not good.'

'Is he dead?'

'Dead right. Perhaps a strategic retreat ...' suggested the Dr. We turned to return, back the way we had come, but more of the silver men were visible coming along the corridor.

'Trapped!' cried the Dr. 'Quick!'

The three of us ducked into the left of the wide ice-chamber, passing in front of the row of advancing robotic soldiers and sprinting away to the side. It was obvious to me at once that there was no way out in this direction.

'What are we going to do?' demanded Linn, as we slid to a halt. 'We can't stay here.'

The menacing-looking, silvery humanoids had wheeled about, and now were advancing upon us in a single rank, marching in perfect step. They moved unhurriedly; implacably; determinedly, deadly-ly. They looked, in fact, like a rank of Nazi stormtroopers parading down Evilstraße, Berlin, in 1938. Except they were all silvery, rather than wearing any kind of black uniform. And that they were marching through a large chamber carved from solid ice, rather than along a city street. And that they wore no insignia, and carried no banners or flags or anything like that. And that they weren't, to be fair, lifting their legs *quite* so high as Nazi stormtroopers might have done. So, on reflection, not *very* like the Nazi stormtroopers then. You see, you need to understand that I chose just now the 'Nazi stormtrooper' analogy to convey their sinister orderliness and threat, rather than wanting to create a whole *visual* picture that would inevitably be more distracting and less expressive.

'Cydermen!' cried the Dr. 'The second most feared evil creature in the galaxy! But what are *they* doing aboard a British experimental naval craft in nineteen-twelve?'

'Cydermen?' I said 'What sort of being might they be?'

'Terrible, implacable creatures,' said the Dr. 'Implacably terrible. Their terror really knows no plac.'

The approaching humanoids were chanting something as they advanced: 'Ooo Aur! ooo aur!'

'What are they saying?' I asked.

'It's their war cry. If I remember correctly, Aur means gold in their language.'

'Gold? That's their *war* cry? – *gold*?'

'It has religious significance for them, I believe,' said the Dr. 'It means they can always believe in their *soul*, and that they have the *power* to *be* ... to be, um, very much like a reactively *inert* and non-corrosive metal.'

'ooo aur!' bellowed the Cydermen, stepping closer with every goosey-gandering step. One of the silvery men lifted his hand. I saw then that it consisted not of fingers and a thumb, but of four silver pistol-barrels and a small thumb-sized cannon. The middle finger detonated, puffing smoke, and the ice-wall behind us burst under brief fire. The ice-chamber rocked, and chunks of ice fell from the ceiling.

'Also,' said the Dr, ducking behind a large ridge of ice

at the far end of the chamber. 'They're allergic to it. Gold, I mean.'

Linn and I were not slow to join him behind the ridge of ice. It was the only cover in the place.

'What kind of creature is allergic to gold?' said Linn. 'Given how perfectly inert and unreactive it is? There's nothing in it to be allergic *to*.'

'A good point,' agreed the Dr. 'Nevertheless, they are. Gold allergic, I mean.'

A second explosion clattered away behind us. Once again, chunks, stalagtites and stalaglufts of ice showered down around us. We were in a situation of some peril.

'Have you *got* any gold?' I asked.

'Not on me,' said the Dr. 'No. Nor, indeed, off me. Neither on me nor off me, do I have any gold. Not really my *style*, gold, now, is it?'

'Linn?' I asked. 'Do *you* have any gold?'

'I'm afraid not,' she replied.

'Well that's not much use,' I pointed out.

'OOO AUR! OOO AUR!' bellowed the advancing Cydermen.

'If we could get some gold, could we stop these Cydermen?' I asked the Dr.

'Easily,' he said.

'And what if we can't get the gold?'

'Then they will be – literally, as well as meta-phorically – unstoppable. They won't stop until we're dead. And, actually, they won't even stop then. They'll carry on after we're dead just as implacably as they are presently doing, before our deaths. Nothing will stop them. In conclusion,' he concluded, 'they won't stop.'

I hazarded a look around the side of the ice ridge behind which we were hiding. The Cydermen were continuing their implacable slow advance, their silver limbs moving with weird machinic co-ordination.

'Do you see their heads?' the Dr asked.

'Yes.' Their crania looked like hard, shiny jar-shaped containers.

'*Slopping* with Cyder,' said the Dr.

'Cyder?'

'The cybernetically enhanced conducting fluid that is the medium of their intelligence. You see, the Cydermen used to be men and women, like you and me. Well, like you, at any rate. But one day, they realised that the jelly-like substance that constitutes naturally occurring organic brains was an inefficient conducting medium for intelligence. The neurones are fixed, trapped in static relation to one another. So the reinvented themselves; reconfigured their brains as a true *fluid*, in which every neurone could connect with every other one as they swirled and swished about – that enables a *huge* number of possible connections, many more than can ever be the case in the normal, *solid* brain tissue. The entire race abandoned their grey-matter brains and uploaded their intellect into the fluid of their jars – a special blend of electrolyte enhancer and accelerant, alcohol-derivative, and an organic-based nutrient solution, derived from some fruit or other I think.'

'It's . . . it's incredible,' I gasped.

'I . . . I know,' said the Dr. 'With the advantage of their new thought-medium their IQs increased a *hundred*fold overnight. It drove them mad . . . for what creature could acquire godlike intellectual and processing powers in an instant and *not* become insane? But their insanity was of a cold, calculating, machinic sort. They reinvented their bodies to be immune to almost all attack, encasing their delicate inner organs in a shell of hard silver. And then, with their invulnerable bodies and their vastly superior medium for thought, these half-human, half-scrumpy creatures began to spread through the galaxy, ruthlessly imposing their caravan-based habitation upon hapless worlds; scooping up whole armies in their monstrous Combine War-Harvesters. The Cydermen!'

'Never mind the history lesson,' urged Linn. 'What are we going to *do*?'

'A good question?'

'And the answer?'

'A *good* answer,' replied the Dr. 'That would be best.'

'And what *is* the good answer?' Linn pressed. 'In this circumstance?'

'I don't know.'

There was another explosion, much closer, and a rain of slush and small pieces of ice rained down upon us. 'But we'd better think of it soon, or we'll be goners. The Cydermen take no prisoners.'

'Think of something, somebody!' I cried. 'Can't you – I don't know – remote-control the TARDY to materialise here, so that we can escape?'

'Nope,' said the Dr. 'Can't do that.'

We were silent for a bit.

'They do seem,' Linn observed, 'to be firing fairly randomly. If they coordinated their fire they could have killed us by now.'

'The cold may be affecting their processing power,' said the Dr. 'Computers. They don't like the cold.'

'They're still coming, though,' I pointed out. 'They'll be on us in a moment.'

Suddenly the gunfire, explosions and the sound of metallic limbs marching on ice ceased. There was complete silence. A man's voice called across the chamber. 'Doctor?'

'I know that voice,' said the Dr. 'But it *can't* be!'

'Doctor! Show yourself! Or I shall have to ask my friends here to eliminate you.'

'It is my nemesis, my adversary!' gasped the Dr. 'The Master Debater!'

This was the first that I had heard of this mysterious and villainous figure; but it was not going to be the last.

'Stand up Doctor,' he boomed. 'And your two companions.'

'We've no choice,' said the Dr. 'We'd better do what he says.'

We stood up.

Standing in the midst of the mass of Cydermen was a tall dark-haired man dressed in black velvet, and sporting an arrowhead-shaped beard on his chin. I mean, I *call* it a beard, but it barely covered the chin. It was more of a beardette. A hemi-beard. A bea. But it was nattily trimmed and sculpted, and it made a nice accompaniment to the black-velvet three-piece and pointy brogues the fellow was wearing. They were exactly the sort of clothes you'd expect an evil genius to wear. It was as if he'd been to a clothes-maker not on *Saville* Row, but on *Eville Row*. Hah! Do you see? D'you see what I did there, with the

joke? That's an example of the sort of joke that sub-
stitutes one word for another than sounds similar but ...
what? What's that?

Alright, alright, I'll stop.

'So, Debater,' declared the Dr. 'We meet yet again.'

'And this time,' the suavely evil figure announced,
'*I* have the upper hand.'

'How did you manage to persuade the Cydermen to
work for you?'

'It's a long story. Too long to go into here, I'm afraid.
Instead of worrying about the hows of the situation,
Doctor, you should be worrying about the imminence of
your own death. Not to mention the deaths of your two
charming companions-stroke-victims, there.'

'But what are you *doing* here?' the Dr demanded. 'On
this prototype British Navy Habbakuk warship?'

'That's another long story,' said the Master Debater.
'Suffice to say that, due to an involved and inter-
connected set of events, I have been deprived of my
TARDY, which has stranded me on this backwater world.
My plan was to use these Cydermen to capture *this* ship,
and then use it to harass the world powers, sink their
navies, that sort of thing. In six months I anticipate
conquering the entire globe. Then I can use its resources,
and direct its best scientific brains, to build me a new
TARDY, and – escape!'

'And what do the Cydermen get from the deal?' the
Dr demanded.

'They get the world when I've finished with it ... a
whole planet to enslave and dominate. But now that
you're here, my dear Doctor, I don't believe I need to go

to the bother of making war on the whole of humanity after all. Instead of conquering this world and enslaving it to make my TARDY I can simply ... steal yours!' He laughed. It was not an attractive laugh. Nor, if I'm honest, was it an especially effective laugh. It didn't capture that penetrating *nya-ha-ha-ha-ha!* laugh that the best evil geniuses have down pat. Instead it was a high-pitched shrieky sort of bray, the sort of noise a very small woman might make if strapped to a kitchen stool and tickled with a feather.

'Steal my TARDY!' exclaimed the Dr. 'Never!'

'I'm afraid you have no choice in the matter. I shall take your TARDY whether you like it or not.'

One of the Cydermen, to the Master Debater's left, spoke up: *'But if you zteal der man here's cra-a-aft and bug-geroff...'* it said, in a raspy metallic burr, *'what shall us do about conquerin' der world and all, oo-aur?'*

'Ooo Aur,' grumbled the ranks of Cydermen, uneasily. *'Ooo. Aur.'*

'Don't be foolish,' said the Master Debater. 'You'll still have control of this warship. You can conquer the planet yourselves. It might take you a *little* longer than it would do if I were here to guide you, what with my tactical brilliance and all. But you'll get there eventually.'

'Oi zuppose so,' said the Cyderman. *'Ooo Aur.'*

'Master Debater!' said the Dr. 'You have surpassed yourself! Or, to be strictly accurate, you have *sub*passed yourself. Which is to say, you have gone *lower* than ever you have before.'

'Give *me* your TARDY!' retorted the Master Debater. 'Never!'

'Then you leave me no choice. Cydergentlemen, fire away.'

All the Cydermen in unison lifted their hands and pointed their finger-clickin' guns in our direction. We three ducked back down behind the ridge. There was a deafening volley of gunshots, mixed with the sound of small cannon fire: smoke and ice engulfed us. Shards and chunks of ice flew through the air.

'We're doomed,' said the Dr.

'We may indeed be,' said Linn. 'Can't either of you think of *anything*?'

There was an especially loud explosion, and larger pieces of ice scattered and rolled. 'Quick,' said the Dr. 'I think they've just blown a hole in the wall behind us ... through it! Quick! Whilst the smoke still covers our retreat!'

We ran as fast as we could, and stumbled through a ragged gap in the ice-wall and into the corridor beyond. Blocks and chunks of ice littered the floor, like scatter-cushions, although markedly less downy or soft. 'Along here!' cried the Dr, running left.

As we sprinted away we heard the voice of the Master Debater behind us: 'but there's nowhere to run *to*, Doctor! We'll catch up with you eventually!'

❖

The corridor led to steps, which brought us to an upper deck. The bodies of British soldiers lay sprawled and scattered all about. 'Back to the TARDY,' I urged. 'Let's get away!'

'It's not as simple as that,' said the Dr. 'If we leave this ice ship floating with its complement of deadly

Cydermen, they almost certainly will indeed over-run the Earth. They're immune to all the weaponry that these humans can muster. It'd be no contest. And an Earth conquered by the Cydermen ... that'd be disastrous. That would completely mess up millions of lives.'

'Surely, and without wishing to sound callous,' I said, panting a little as we ran, 'that's *their* problem, not ours?'

'It'll alter the timelines. The Cydermen aren't supposed to conquer the Earth in the twentieth-century. Not until the beginning of the twenty-first.'

'So some time lines get a little kinked ...' I said.

'It'd mean *you'll* both cease to exist, for instance,' the Dr said. 'Both of you. You see, you were both born on Earth *after* this event.'

'We really must defeat these Cydermen,' I said. 'We can't leave Earth to its terrible fate.'

We reached the bridge.

It had obviously seen some fighting since we had last been there: the teak was scorched, and water pooled on the icy floor. The Commodore and his helmsman were both lying face down.

'Poor souls!' cried the Dr. '*Mortem*, and without leaving their posts.'

'Unless you want to join them,' said Linn. 'We'd better think quick.'

Behind us we could hear the war-chant of the Cyderman, getting implacably and horribly closer. Ooo Aur. Ooo Aur. OOO AUR.

'There!' said the Dr triumphantly, pointing through the navigation slit at the front of the bridge. 'You see that ship?'

It was the profile of a mighty liner, visible against the black sky by virtue of its glittery banks of illuminated portholes, and its gaily lit upper decks. Its four fat funnels blocked out the starlight, passing bales of smoke up into the cold night air.

'We'll contact them,' the Dr said. 'Recruit them ... as reinforcements.'

'Recruit them *how*?' I boggled.

'Tell them the truth! They can send people aboard *this* craft. It looks like an affluent ship: they'll surely have gold. *That's* what we need to defeat the Cydermen – gold.'

'So,' I summarised. 'You're suggesting we radio a strange ship, tell them that we're the only survivors aboard a secret Naval experiment that nobody has ever heard of, and that they must come aboard *with all their gold* to help us fight a race of implacable cyborg creatures who otherwise will conquer the Earth?'

'Yes!'

'There's the chance,' I said, '—and I appreciate that it's only a chance – that they *might not* believe us.'

'The future of the whole world is at stake! They *must* help!'

'The radio,' said Linn, 'is broken, I'm afraid.'

The Dr and I looked at the radio. It was a charred mass of twisted metal and burnt wood.

'There's nothing for it,' cried the Dr, grabbing the ship-steering-wheel-y-thing and hauling it as far to starboard as it would go. Or to port. I've never, if I'm being honest, been quite sure which is which when it comes to those two directions.

'Doctor! What are you doing!'

'It's our only chance. I'll pull this ship across their bows. Bump into them, if necessary, to attract their attention.'

'Are you sure?' I asked. 'And by *sure* I mean, *absolutely insane*?'

'Certainly not,' said the Dr. 'Drastic measures are called for. The fate of the whole world is in the balance.'

We all three of us peered through the forward viewing hatch.

'We seem to be powering directly towards the ship now,' said Linn.

'So we do,' agreed the Dr. 'Well, the rudder is hard down, as far as it will go. I suspect that we'll keep turning, and pass in front of their bows soon.'

We stared anxiously forward.

'We *seem*,' said Linn again, 'to be heading straight for them still.'

'Hmm,' said the Dr. 'That does seem to be the case.'

'Doctor . . .' I said, increasingly alarmed. From behind us the *ooo aur! ooo aur!* chanting was becoming everlouder.

'This Habbakuk-type ship seems to be much less manoeuvrable,' said the Dr, in a worried voice, 'than I had anticipated. Perhaps we should . . .' and he seized hold of the steery-wheely-circle again. 'Ah,' he said. 'This seems to be . . . more . . . sort of . . .uh! *uh*!'—he was heaving with all his might—'stuck,' he concluded.

We were almost upon the hapless other ship.

'Watch out!' cried Linn. But it was no use.

With a massive shuddering cacophonous crunch we

collided with the mystery ship, careering into its side in a glancing but nevertheless catastrophic blow. I was knocked from my feet and slipped about in the cold pools of the bridge floor. The whole structure trembled and shook, and a rain of ice chunks plummeted from the ceiling.

The Dr was supporting himself by clinging onto the big steering wheel. I hauled myself to my feet hand over hand on one of the consoles, barely keeping upright as the bridge shimmied and shook. Straight ahead I saw the black flank of the other craft sliding past us, close enough to touch.

And then the shuddering stopped, and we were floating free again.

Linn screamed, pointing to the door.

Behind us the Cydermen were crowding in at the entrance to the bridge. 'Oo Aur!' they bellowed, levelling their guns at us.

'We're doomed!' cried the Dr. 'Hide!'

Then everything happened very quickly. The three of us jumped behind the steering column. The leading Cyderman fired a volley from his thumb, and it thudded into the floor of the bridge a few metres in front of us, exploding in a violent burst that turned the pools of water to steam, and sent shards and shrapnel of ice spraying everywhere. Then there was a moment's silence, just enough to hear a deep, distant groan pass through the fabric of the ship, a vast deep sound like a gigantic beast moaning in pain. Then – like a giant diamond crystal struck in *exactly* the right place by the jeweller's hammer – the mighty craft began to split.

Jarred and sheared by the impact with the mystery ocean liner, this explosion (to the front of and along the dead centre of the craft) proved the tipping point. A crack spread the length of the bridge. In moments it widened, gaping and parting for all the world like a huge grin. 'Hold on!' shouted the Dr as the ice groaned and heaved. We clung together, and felt the angle of the bridge floor tip as the left side separated from the right. The *oo-aur*s of the Cydermen had taken on alarmed tones, and then everything was blotted out by a massive crumbling roaring symphony of structural collapse.

The floor rocked left, tipped right, rocked left again and finally turned through ninety degrees, sloughing us all off. We fell into the blackness of night, plummeting through cold air until we struck the icy black water with a swallowing splash of cold agony. The water felt like it was cutting all parts of my body at once. It was bitterly and agonizing cold.

Momentarily we were submerged, and I felt my chest constrict. Then we broke the surface, still all clinging together, gasping and crying.

I blinked the seawater from my eyes, and tried to look around. The two portions of the *Icetanic* were falling away from us on either side, rotating slowly in the choppy water as they searched for their new points of flotational equilibrium. The swell from this motion buoyed us up. The twin halves of the ship slid and rolled steadily away from us.

'The cold!' cried Linn. 'The water is so *cold*!'

Then I saw the Cydermen. They were tumbling from the slippery ice, shelled out of the internal chambers and caverns of the mighty ice-structure like peas from a great white pod. The distant calls of '*Ooo! Aur!*' were cut short with *gloop!* and *glurg!* noises, and then they disappeared.

They were all falling into the freezing waters and sinking into its depths.

'What,' I gasped, through chattering teeth, 'what will happen to them?'

The Dr was treading water by kicking his legs in froggy motions. 'Straight to the bottom,' he said, grimly.

'Will they drown?'

'Dear me no,' said the Dr. 'They're far too toughly designed to *drown*.'

'Well – will the pressure down there kill them?'

'Certainly not. They'll gather themselves and start walking – slowly but surely – for the shore.'

'Then the Earth is doomed!' I moaned. 'We have failed!'

'Well,' said the Dr, kicking more furiously as the swell dipped us all down, 'I don't think so. They'll all be dead long before they *reach* the shore, you see.'

'But how?' I gasped.

'The sea water of course,' snapped the Dr. 'It'll poison them. They'll be walking through a fatal medium.'

'I thought you said that only gold could kill them?'

'That's quite right. There's a surprisingly large amount of gold dissolved in the ocean, you know. Approaching two milligrams per tonne. And if that doesn't sound like a lot, then consider how many tonnes of seawater there are in the world . . . something like one and a third billion cubic kilometres of the stuff. The Cydermen will have to march through billions of tonnes of the stuff, and all that gold will accumulate in their chest-grills. They're doomed.'

'That's good news,' I said. Actually what I said was *thththats gg ggg ggood n-news attshOOO!*. But I feel sure the Dr and Linn understood me.

'What about the ship we hit?' asked Linn.

The swell carried us up, and we caught a glimpse of the mystery ship over the top of the still slowly tumbling right-side half of the *Icetanic*. It was sailing away, apparently unharmed. 'Looks alright, don't you think?' said the Dr.

'I suppose so. But what about *us*?'

'I think we need to find the . . . ah *there* we go – there she is: the TARDY!'

'Can the TARDY float?' I asked, shiveringly. I was thinking how very heavy it must be.

'When you consider the relationship between the compact external shape of the thing, and the amount of air *inside* the structure,' said the Dr, 'the TARDY may well be the most buoyant object in the history of the universe.'

'I hadn't thought of it like that,' I said.

'Come on.'

We broke apart, and swam, our limbs aching with the ferocity of the cold, towards a rectangular shape. The Dr was right: it was so buoyant, in fact, that it was in effect *standing on top* of the water. We opened the door and crawled up onto the floor inside, shivering and soaking but alive.

It was a relief beyond words to shut the door on that freezing environment.

'Let's get out of here,' said the Dr, pulling towels from the central console and passing them around. 'I do believe we've done what we came to do ... averted catastrophe once again.'

PROLOGUE

Time.

Have you ever really *thought* about it? Neither had I, until I met the Dr.

What is time? Whither time? Whence? Thither or hence? Who knows? And whom? And *why* does Whom know?

What?

Hold up: go back a mo. Start again.

Let us define time. Time is the difference between a hot cup of coffee and a cold cup of coffee. It is the difference between a cold beer on a hot day, and a *warm* beer on a hot day. It turns young to old, and via the mystery of parturition it turns old into young. It's what makes yesterday different to today: it's the difference, in other words, between yester and to. Since to is the opposite of fro, it follows that yester and fro are the same thing. Yesterfro. What am I talking about?

Time will tell.

Time *began* at the *beginning*. This is why, strictly speaking, we should call it the *beganning*.

Time is a dimension.

But (and pay close attention, for this bit is really *really* important) – even though it is a dimension, Time is *not* space. This is because one day *in time* you will die. That's coming closer and closer, I'm sorry to say. You can't avoid it by moving around in space. You can't take three steps to the left and watch your death slide past you, shaking its fist in impotent rage like a bobsleigh-man who's lost control of the steering. It doesn't work like that. Time is a *two*-dimensional, not a three-dimensional, thing. You can move along it from *before* to *after*, and if you're clever enough you can move from *after* to *before*. But you can't go sideways in time.

On the other hand, you *can* go sideways in space. I'll prove it

There!

What do we deduce from this? That *spacetime*, the theory advanced by Albert Einstein, is erroneously mistaken. You see, time is a *different sort of thing* from space. This is a really important point in the story I'm about to tell. I'd like you to bear it in mind, if you can.

Who am I?

My name is Prose Tailor. I tailor prose, I cut it to shape, fit it together. This prose you're reading now is my work. I was a companion of the Dr. *The* Dr – that's right. Him. I was there when he uncovered the essential mystery at the heart of the cosmos, the answer to the big question. I saw with my own eyes the solution.

You are about to read my story.

＊

The Dr belonged to that ancient race of beings called the Time Gentlemen. Alone of all the myriad races of the galaxy these austere and wise beings possessed a degree of mastery over time. Not a master's degree, neither, but a PhD, and sometimes even postdoctoral qualifications. The most important time of my life was spent in the company of one of these Time Gentlemen, known as The Dr.

It is the duty of the Time Gentlemen to protect the grammar of time.

You didn't realise that time has a *grammar*? Ah, you deluded and ignorant fool. To master time, you need to understand the difference between a time noun and a time verb, a time subject and a time object. You need to understand tense and mood without getting tense or moody. Time is things happening in a particular order, according to a particular system of rules. Start breaking those rules and soon the whole fabric of time would unravel. The morrow would not longer follow the day; the day would not longer follow the yester. The yes. I mean yesterday. With the result that yesterday might come after tomorrow, and everybody would get very confused. The processes of life would break down; thought itself would become meandering and untenable.

'Time is *story*,' the Dr said to me once. 'It's a narrative. If the narrative gets all tangled up, then the story becomes impossible to follow. That's why the Time Gentlemen are so important. Because we preserve the proper line of the story.'

Here is a story. A child is born on Earth of the twenty-third century. And who is this child?

It's me, of course.

I grew to adulthood in *You-'K?*, a small country that is part of the continent of *You-Rapper!*, itself merely a component of the World Wide Federation of Hip Humanity, our glorious global government. After school I went to the Prose College where I learned to shape, snip and tailor prose. After my graduation I worked as a prose tailor, out of a little shop in the Reefer Barn (the main mall for all You-Rapper's Reefer needs). It was tough work. Few people in You-'K? have any use for prose. Of course, state regulation requires every citizen to possess a dozen personalised lyrics by the age of majority, and *Rap* Tailors do good business. But I never had the knack for rap. I was rap-knack-less. My parents were ashamed to see me follow the ignominious path of the Prose Tailor, writing little pieces of legalese, or perhaps the liner notes for other people's albums. I barely earned a living: money was always tight, and I never had enough for the little luxuries that make existence bearable. Worst of all I never had enough cash to be able to *travel* ... to voyage to far countries, as I dreamed of doing! To visit the home of our Global religion, the great nation of *You-Say!*, the holy land, where the power of sayin' was first mooted – where it was first determined that every ordinary person, no matter how inarticulate, ugly or stoopid, could have their say. But I would never be able to see that exotic land nor travel to the Progrok paradise of *Rush?Yeah!*, nor the teetering, foul-mouthed antipodian continent of '*Oz*' – *Ausbourneia*.

My life was trapped in narrow grooves. Waking, working, eating, sleeping.

And then one day I answered an advertisement for assistant-stroke-companion to a Time Gentleman, and everything about my life changed.

My life, up until that moment, had been empty. I shuffled to work and shuffled home alone at the end of the day. My days were without colour; my life was as hopeless as a soap-on-a-rope that has lost its soap and is only rope thereby becoming hopeless *as* soap in the shower. You can't wash yourself in rope, after all. *I* was ropey.

As you can see from this, I've never been a very *good* prose tailor.

Until I joined the Dr and his apprentice, Linnaeus Trout. The three of us together had a series of extraordinary adventures. And ultimately I was with him when he discovered the secret at the heart of time; and fate – in the shape of a malign ET and his Dr-killing weapon – forced us apart.

This is my story.

Chapter Seven

THE DR RE-UN-DEGENERATES

But although I was anxious that the Dr was injured, perhaps fatally, in fact things took a much stranger path. Not to put too fine a point on it: I was privileged to witness one of the Dr's 're-new-generative episodes'. You see, unlike most other life-forms the Time Gentlemen do not die. At least, they don't die in the normal course of things. Instead their bodies 're-un-degenerate'. One 'incarnation', or 'iteration', or 'actor playing' the Dr passes away, and an entirely new one takes its place. I *know*! It's almost too incredible. It's almost *beyond* belief. But there you go.

I watched as the Dr fell to the floor, although not so carelessly as he was likely actually to injure himself. He lay there, and his face went all – fuzzy. I can't think of a better way of describing it. For a moment it looked as though he possessed two faces, but then his features settled into a new configuration. His hair took on the lifeless, shaggy appearance of a bad wig, and then it too seemed to disappear revealing a short crew cut. The Dr had changed into a tall, bony man with a large nose.

He sat up. 'Ey-oop,' he declared.

'Doctor ....?' I hazarded.

''Appen Taylor! Ey-oop Linn!' he said, clambering to his feet. 'Oo I *say!*'

'Doctor! You're alright!'

He nodded, smiled, and then a look of concern crossed his face. He burped, noisily. 'I'm terribly sorry,' he said. 'I do apologise.' Again he belched. A sour smell of egg-nog became palpable in the air of the TARDY. 'You have to understand,' said the Dr, embarrassed, 'that the process of re-un-degeneration carries with it some —' He burped again.

'Some?

'Some difficulties. My body has *changed*, you see.'

'Doctor what's happened?' I cried. 'I was sure you'd *died*!'

'No, no. Almost impossible to kill me. Instead of regular death, my body re-*un*-degenerates. What this means is that all the cells that make up my body change. Anything imprinted with my DNA becomes part of a different body.'

'But your DNA ... it's not human ...' I said, trying to grasp the enormity of what I had witnessed.

'Of course not,' said the Dr. 'It's Time Gentlemen DNA. But it's there, in every cell, and during the process of re-new-generation it undergoes a sort of shimmy, or cataleptic shudder, and it marks out a new form for the body. But, you see, not *everything* in my body contains my DNA. That's just as true of me as it is of you.'

'Really? You mean there are cells in my body that don't even contain my DNA?' asked Linn.

'Of course,' said the Dr, his skin acquiring a rather green tinge. 'For instance, your gut flora. Now, you need your gut flora to digest your food. It's a thoroughly necessary thing. But the bacteria out of which one's gut flora are composed carry their own, independent DNA. They are fine-tuned to existing in the set up of their host's body, and when that body radically changes they ... don't like it. Stomach-upsets, diarrhoea and nausea are the *least* of the symptoms.'

'What was the business with the "ey oop" and the "'appen" when you came round from your trance?' I asked.

'A momentary grammatical aberration,' said the Dr, looking distinctly queasy. If you'll excuse me, I must rush to the toilet.' He hauled himself to his feet and ran from the control room, making a series of repeated *bluuerCA'H*! noises as he went.

✱

After a half hour or so in which Linn and I did nothing but idle around the control room, peering at the gleaming controls and trying to make small-talk, the Dr re-emerged from the toilet. The intervening period had been marked by the background noise of a grown man attempting, apparently, to force his spleen up through his throat and out into the toilet pan by using the muscles of his diaphragm alone. It was not a pretty sound.

'There,' said the Dr, looking pale. 'I think that's got that sorted out. Better out than in, I suppose. I do apologise for that. It's the cerum aerobic bacteria in the lower gut that ... mostly ... oh no.' He put his hand to his mouth and his cheeks ballooned out like a jazz trumpeter's. 'Excuse mee*eurrkh*,' he blurted.

He rushed from the control room.

Once again Linn and I sat in the control room, looking pointedly in other directions than one another's faces.

From time to time we made eye contact and smiled, weakly, at one another. 'Well,' I said, at one point. 'This is all very interesting, isn't it.' And she replied, 'yes, it is.' I asked, 'have you seen him do this before, then?' and she replied, 'no, actually, not,' and I said, 'ah!' We sat in silence for a while. All the time, however, we were accompanied by a cacophonous soundtrack of what sounded like a pig trying to give birth to a much larger, and much more noisily unhappy, pig in the next room.

Eventually the noises died away and the Dr emerged, even paler than before but wearing a brave smile.

'Again I apologise,' he said. 'It is an unfortunate side-effect of the DNA mutation, the broad-spectrum change of cellular germ plasm impacts very sharply upon the gut flora, with concomitant isolation of the Lactobacillus plantarum and an anti-Candida emetic that involves certain projectile gut-spasm implications,' said the Dr, in a sober voice. 'Also I was puking like a dog.'

'We heard,' said Linn.

'Anyway, anyway, anyway,' said the Dr, trying to rally the situation by smacking his hands together and rubbing the palms up against one another. 'It's all behind me now. At least it will be, as soon as my lower bowel catches up with the more immediate negative reaction of the stomach and intestinal changes. But we don't want to worry about that now. We need to get *on*.'

Chapter Three

THE TIME GENTLEMEN'S
CONVENANCE

We stepped through into the meeting chamber. It was a splendidly appointed and decorated chamber; every surface was either gilded, silvered or bronzed: except for the floor which was decorated with verdigris, or 'verdigreased' as the phrase goes. On tiered platforms arranged in a horseshoe shape about the central podium as many as a hundred Time Gentlemen were sitting on their official benches. When I say 'as many as a hundred' I mean 'as few as a hundred', which is to say, a hundred. There was a distinctly pompous and official air.

'Right, you two,' the Dr said to us. 'Best behaviour, alright? This is an *official* Time Gentlemen's Convenance. It's not a place for mucking-about-in. Not,' he corrected himself, glancing about himself nervously as if conscious that the grammatical exactitude expected of all Time Gentlemen applied most particularly in this space, 'not an environment in which mucking can be allowed about.' He looked at the floor and tried one more time. 'Not about *in of which*, there can, now, be allowed, any mucking.'

'We understand,' said Linn.

'Convenance?' I queried.

'What?'

'You sure that's a word?'

'Of course I am.'

The Dr bowed to the Time Chairgentleman, seated at apex of the many curving rows of seats, behind the sumptuous Time Table of Garlicfree. We both followed suit. Then we made our way to the side of the chamber and slid onto one of the benches.

'You're *quite* sure?' I pressed. 'I mean ... convenance. It doesn't have the ...'

'It is a meeting *convened* by the Time Gentlemen. Therefore it is a Time Gentlemen's *Convenance*.'

'It's just that I've never,' I said, a little nervously. 'I mean, in all my years as a tailor of prose, I can say that —'

'Shhhpshh!' hushed the Dr crossly. 'Tsschh! Czsch!'

The Chair had got to his feet. Which is to say, the Time Gentleman chairing the meeting, who had been sitting in a chair, was now standing. The chair itself remained standing throughout the whole proceedings. 'Time Gentlemen and honoured guests!' he commenced. 'It is with enormous, Gentlemen's, *relish* that I welcome the Doctor to our proceedings.'

'Too kind,' murmured the Dr, bowing his head to the gathering.

'As many of you know,' said the Chair. 'The Doctor has been engaged on a certain secret mission – the nature of which I cannot, in the present company, disclose. This mission is of the *utmost importance*. It is, in other words, *more* than most important. There is an *ut* involved too.' A murmur went through the room. 'Suffice to say,' boomed the Chair. 'That his mission has been more than a standard Time Gentlemen mission – more than going about painting-in the missing apostrophes from shop-signs, and more than correcting complete strangers on their failure to use the subjunctive mode.'

'If I *were*,' murmured the entire room. 'If I *were* ...'

'No. Our intelligence informs us that a TGV has been purchased by a mysterious and malefactoral figure in Le Bar Sexy in sector Parsec-"C" out by the Giffin Head Nebula.'

'A TGV!' whispered the assembled Time Gentlemen.

'I need not tell you how serious this matter is,' said the Chair. 'The one thing that can destroy the life of a Time Gentleman ... and it could be used again and again, perhaps to wipe out the entire race of the Time Gentlemen.'

'Blime-crikey!' said the Dr.

'Our intelligence reports,' said the Chair, 'that ... and I ask you all to prepare for a shock ... but that the gun is now in the possession of ... Stavros.'

The whole room fell silent with shock.

'I'm afraid so,' said the Chair, sombrely. 'I hardly need to tell you how serious a development this is. If Stavros is able to arm his evil cyborg army with TGVs, then the whole future of Time Gentlemanliness is in danger. We could all be wiped out!'

'What can we do!'

'For now,' said the Chair, 'continue with your various missions. We have breaches of time-grammar that need clearing up in every sector of the Galaxy. Meanwhile the Council of Time Gentlemen will ponder our options. We may be compelled to take the most drastic course of action of all – going back in time to before Stavros was able to create his monstrosities, and eliminating them before they are even created!'

There was only one item of 'any other business', relating to the washrooms. After that the meeting was adjourned.

Chapter Six

THE SLUTTYTEENS

The TARDY rematerialised on the patch of green lawn just outside the Houses of Parliament in London, England, Europe, the World, Solar System. The date was 1960. It was a bright sunny day.

'So what's the problem here?' Linn was asking as we stepped from the TARDY. Red Routemaster double-decker buses rolled past. Beefeaters walked arm-in-arm with soldiers in busbies. Everybody was wearing mini-skirts, driving mini-cars, and laughing with mini-hahas.

'It's like a history lesson!' I exclaimed.

'Lesson in ahistory,' Linn said darkly. 'More like.'

I smiled at this, and even forced out a chuckle, but then I gave up. 'No, I don't get that at all.'

'Never mind.'

'Come along,' said the Dr. 'We've a job to do. The government here has been infiltrated,' the Dr said. 'An alien race called the Sluttyteens. They look on the outside like obese teenagers. But that's just a prosthetic skin-suit. Underneath that skin, gleaming as it is with the oil of sebum, are pure Slutties, from the planet Slut.' The Dr shook his head. 'Very nasty types. No class or style at all.'

'They shouldn't be here?'

'Indeed not. That's a clear violation of the law of temporal enclitic participles, right there. They shouldn't be on this planet at all. They should just go back to the planet Slut, and grow up. If we were to do nothing they'd use their hidden positions to pass a series of laws liberalising sexual behaviour, turning nineteen-sixties Britain into a louche and swinging place with no respect of any kind for order, grammar, sequentiality or anything at all. They must be stopped!'

'How?'

'Should be easy enough. I'll slip into the main chamber of Parliament, whilst a governmental debate is going on. I'll walk up to the Minister for Swinging Affairs, and yank off her skin-suit – in full view of everybody. Once they're exposed, it'll be a simple matter to chase them back to their homeworld.'

'Shall we come with you?' I asked.

'Nah,' said the Dr. 'I'll be fine by myself. It should only take me a minute.' He marched off for the main entrance of the House of Commons.

❋

It was a warm and sunshiny day, and it was pleasant to sit on the grass with Linn at my side.

'Linn,' I said, plucking strands of grass and twirling them between my fingertips. 'Now that the Dr's away for a moment, can I confess something to you?'

'Go on.'

'Promise not to tell him?'

'Alright.'

'I know how important grammar and everything is to you. And I know I'm a prose tailor and everything. But the thing is ... '

'What?'

'I can never remember when to use *who* and when to use *whom*,' I said. 'Frankly, I can't understand why we have both those words. We could just make do with *who* and everybody would still understand everybody.'

'Maybe they would,' Linn agreed. 'But then we could probably understand one another if we did away with all grammatical tense, all distinction between subject and object ... why, we could probably point and grunt and get our message across. But it wouldn't be a very elegant or sophisticated universe, then, would it?'

'No need to be snarky,' I said.

'Tell me, Prose. Do you understand the difference between *he* and *him*?'

'Um,' I said.

'She punched *he* in the face? Or: she punched *him* in the face?'

'The second one.'

'And you know the difference between *she* and *her*.' Linn pressed. 'It's just like *he* and *him*, after all. He disappointed *she*? Or: he disappointed *her*?'

'Well,' I said. 'Yes.'

'Well, in that case you already understand the difference between *who* and *whom*,' she said. 'It's exactly the same thing. I really don't understand why people have such a problem with it. You wouldn't say *I gave the book to he*, would you! You wouldn't say *he kissed she*. No. You wouldn't. In exactly the same way you wouldn't ask *to who did he give the book*? Of course not. To *whom* did he give the book. He was the one to *whom* the book was given.'

'Is it really as simple as that?'

'It really is.'

'I feel like I've learned something here today,' I said.

'Here comes the Doctor,' said Linn, getting to her feet. 'And he's walking funny.'

❖

He was indeed walking in a most peculiar manner, taking strides with his right foot and them making little hoppy-draggy motions with his left to catch up. He was clutching his gut. 'Something's wrong,' Linn said, hurrying over to him.

'Help me inside the TARDY,' he said, in a strangulated voice.

'What happened?' I asked, taking some of his weight as he struggled over the grass. 'Did you expose the overweight minister as a Sluttyteen in a skin-suit?'

'Not exactly,' gasped the Dr.

'Then what?'

'Well – I managed to get in the chamber alright, and sidle up to the Minister. But no matter how vigorously I tugged away at her fat-suit it wouldn't come off. It was only when she was rolling around on the floor shouting, with me on top of her, and an enormous commotion all around us, that I realised she wasn't a Sluttyteen at all. Just an amply-proportioned middle-aged woman. I think I'd picked the wrong one.'

'So what happened then?'

'What happened then,' said the Dr, as we opened the door of the TARDY, 'was that special branch shot me.'

'Shot you?' I gasped.

'That's right. Shot me in the gut. Can't say I blame

them. We'd better get out of here before the army turns up.'

He staggered inside the TARDY, fell against the console, pressed buttons to dematerialise us, and then, with a gasp, he fell to the floor.

'Doctor!' I cried, running over to him. 'Are you alright?'

'Not so much alright' he said, 'as *dying*.' And on that last word, he passed out.

Chapter Nine

BETRAYAL!

'For the *last* time,' said the Dr, tetchily. 'It was an *accident*. Come come *come*, how was I to know? It could have happened to anybody!'

'Dead! Dead!' I wailed. 'The woman of my dreams!'

'There's no point in getting so wound-up about it,' said the Dr. 'I can't believe you're blaming me for that ... can't you see how irrational that is? Can't you see that I really had nothing to do with it?'

'He does have a point,' said Linn.

But my grief was making me blind.

'You have to understand that everybody dies,' the Dr said. 'It's the way of things.'

'It's all very well for *you* to say that!' I said. 'If you die you just pop back to life with nothing but an upset tummy. It's not so easy for the likes of *us*.'

'Well,' said the Dr, looking around him in a faintly senile manner. 'I wouldn't describe re-un-de as easy. My dear fellow,' he added, kindly. 'You do look upset!'

'Can you blame me?' I cried.

'Of course not. Nobody blames you. Why don't you take a seat, maybe have a cup of tea? You'll feel better in a moment.'

'My heart is shattered into a googolplex of pieces!' I snapped.

'There there,' he offered, vaguely.

'Doctor,' said Linn. 'Not to ignore Prose's sufferings, but: we still have our mission, don't we. And if we can't go *outside* . . .'

'It's a puzzler,' agreed the Dr.

'There must be a solution.'

'Hey, I'm in emotional *pain* over here,' I cried.

'Have you any ideas?'

'I was thinking,' said the Dr. 'I *could* send out my robot dog, K2. He could fetch the device, and suffer no ill-effects.'

'You have a robot dog?'

'Yes! Well, sort of. Or, to speak absolutely accurately—'

'Yes?'

'In *absolutely* accurate terms, no not really. He's a little less a robot dog, and a little more, strictly speaking, the second-highest mountain peak on Earth.'

'You keep the second-highest mountain peak on Earth aboard the TARDY?'

'I put it in the dog kennel.'

'The TARDY has a dog kennel?'

'From the outside it's kennel-sized. On the inside it's large enough to accommodate – well, the entire mountain.'

'I don't understand why you'd detach the Earth's second highest mountain and put it inside the TARDY.'

'*I* didn't detach it,' said the Dr. 'It detached itself. It was never a real mountain in the first place. It was a mountain-sized robot pet from a planet inhabited by a race of particularly large rocky aliens. I won't bore you with the story of how it ended up on earth, or why I gave it sanctuary aboard the TARDY. Suffice to say that it involved me saving the Earth from certain destruction.'

'But— has nobody noticed that you've removed the Earth's second tallest peak?'

'Who'd notice? A few dozen mountaineers. Nobody else. And who pays any attention to them?'

'But surely they would raise the alarm?'

'They travel all the way to Tibet to climb this mountain. When they get there they discover that it's actually a small hillock about ten feet high. What do you think they're going to do? Go back and make a big fuss? Or climb straight to the top, have their photo taken, and then trot back down and spend the rest of the expedition playing PS3? The latter, of course. That way they can boast that they climbed K2 in record time.'

I could stand it no longer. I got to my feet and rushed from the control room, dashing down the corridor in search of a room where I could be alone with my misery.

※

I stumbled into the TARDY's extensive car-parking facility, a room just large enough to take a narrow single bed. On this I flung myself, and abandoned myself to my grief.

After a while, as my sobs died away, I thought I heard something.

'Hello?' came a voice. It sounded tinny, distant, like a voice over a crystal radio set.

'What?' I snapped. 'Who's that? What?'

'To whom do I have the pleasure of speaking—?'

'Leave me alone!'

'Is that the handsome young male assistant to the Doctor?' asked the voice.

My curiosity was engaged just enough to overcome my self-pity. I looked around the tiny room: four grey walls, a grey ceiling; a bed (nothing underneath it; I checked). There was nowhere for another person to hide. 'Who *is* this?'

'I am the Master Debater,' declared the voice. As soon as he said it, I thought to myself: I knew I recognised the voice.

'Didn't we abandon you upon Earth in nineteen-twelve?' I said.

'Indeed you did. In the freezing waters of the North Atlantic. Hardly polite.'

'But I suppose you have your own TARDY.'

'Indeed.'

'And how are you able to speak to me now?'

'I've patched an audio-communication through the TARDY's control panel.'

'You've done *what*?'

'It's a complicated business, and one that would take me too long to explain fully.'

'What do you want?'

'I need your help,' said the Master Debater.

'Why should I help you?' I asked. 'You are the Evil Time-gentleman.'

'Why should you help the *Doctor*?' the ET countered. 'He killed the woman you loved.'

I was silent for ten or fifteen seconds. 'You know about that,' I said.

'I told you ... I've been in effect bugging the TARDY

via a device lodged in its Hyperspatial Scanner. I over-heard the whole of that last conversation with the Doctor. Right now I've rechannelled a viral subroutine through to the intercom located by the door. I can't talk for long: the TARDY's own antiviral programmes will locate this link soon enough and wipe it out.'

I sat up. My heart was fierce with rage. 'What do you want me to do?' I asked. 'Understand: I'm not saying that I will do this thing ... whatever it may be. But I am only asking. What do you want of me?'

'I just need to know what the Time Gentlemen Convenance told you.'

'That's all?'

'That's all.'

'What's in it for you?'

'That's my business,' said the tinny little voice. Then there was a tinny little laugh. 'But after all, I *am* a Time Gentleman. It's hardly *my* fault that they've barred me from their meetings.'

'Weren't you banned for acts of unspeakable evil, or something?' I said.

'Or something,' he agreed. 'But if the Convenance has *agreed* something, then I need to know about it.'

'I don't see how it could do any harm to tell you,' I said, a little uncertainly. 'They announced they'd discovered a TGV.'

'A Time Gentleman Violator!' exclaimed the Master Debater's suave voice. 'How shocking. Did they say whom had obtained this device?'

'They said something about Stavros.'

'Oo, how terrible. If he arms his cyborg army with

such weapons,' the Master Debater said, thoughtfully, 'then the entire race of Time Gentlemen is doomed!'

'That was pretty much the gist of the meeting.'

'That means me too, you know. That doomed encompasses me as well.'

'I suppose so.'

'Well, don't you think it was pretty unsporting of the Convenance to keep me in the dark about this news?'

'Look,' I said, feeling uneasy. 'I'm not sure I should even be talking to you ... I mean, aren't you the Doctor's arch enemy?'

'Well, yes I am. But it's only a small arch. If I were the Convenance,' he went on, 'I'd send the Doctor back on a mission to before Stavros was able to create his robots, and prevent them ever coming about!'

'I don't think I can say—' I said.

'You don't need to say anything! Don't worry, my dear fellow,' said the Master Debater's voice, growing fainter. 'I wouldn't want you to feel that you had in any way *betrayed* your Doctor ...'

And with that he was gone.

✳

I made my way back to the control room of the TARDY with a slow and rather shuffling step. My mind was undecided. Could I truly betray the Dr? He had never intended to cause me the hurt that had come my way. But on the other hand ... my mind kept returning to the last time I had seen *her* face.

Inside the control room, the Dr was at the console. 'Ah!' he said, cheerily. 'Feeling better.'

'Yes,' I said, in a weak voice. Now that I was with him

again, I felt guilty about my conversation with the Master Debater. Had I said more than I ought? Should I tell the Dr about it? 'I'm,' I hazarded. 'I'm sorry for my behaviour earlier.'

'Don't mention it. We've just had new orders from the Time Gentleman's Convenance. We're to abandon this mission and zoop on back to the Planet Skary.'

'The Planet Skary?' I queried.

'Zoop?' Linn queried.

'Yep. We're to stop Stavros before he can create an entire race of merciless cyborgs and arm them with the only weapon capable of destroying the Time Gentlemen!'

Chapter Five

THE NEAR MAGICAL
DISAPPEARANCE OF THE WATER
INTO THE TARDY TOWELS

It took the Dr a while to recover enough clean towels so that we could dry ourselves properly. Linn and I stood there as he rummaged through the cupboard in the central console, icy water from the North Atlantic of 1912 dripping off our bodies onto the floor of the TARDY's control room.

'Here you both are,' he said finally, bringing out two large blue towels. I held mine in front of me before starting to rub myself with it, and saw that it carried the words TARDY OFFICIAL TOWEL PRODUCT upon it. 'Official towels?'

'Yes.'

'You have *official* towels?'

'Oh I *do*.'

'Is there, what, like a *complete range* of merchandise, or something?'

'Just the towels. And,' he added, paddling his fingers in amongst the line of his necktie, and looking therefore not unlike Oliver Hardy as he did so, 'this natty necktie.' The tie was black, with a rectangular blue shape upon it. 'But the towels are super, aren't they? You'll find,' he went on, rather smugly, 'that they can absorb almost unlimited amounts of water without getting damp.'

I gave the towel a try, and soon discovered that he spoke the truth: no matter how sopping I was, the towel sucked up the water and still felt dry to the touch. 'It's like magic,' exclaimed an impressed Linn. 'How does it work?'

'Ah,' said the Dr, sagely, applying the towel to his own prodigious hairdo. 'It's all part of the marvellous operation of the TARDY ... one more example of the futuristic technology that has kept the Time Gentlemen ahead of the game—'

'And how about hot chocolate?' Linn demanded. 'You got any marvellous machinery in this spaceship for making *that*?'

*

'So, this Master-chappy,' I asked, once we were all dry. The one who was in charge of all those Cydermen back on the *Icetanic*.'

'Yes?'

'I was just wondering who we were dealing with back there, that's all.'

'Whom,' corrected the Dr.

'Whom.'

'You were wondering,' said the Dr pedantically, '*with whom* we were dealing.'

'So,' I started again, cautiously, '*whom* is he, exactly?'

'Who is he,' corrected Linn.

'What I mean,' I said, 'is that you sounded pretty surprised to see him. I'm wondering whether you had any suspicions as whether *he* was the one who, or whom, either really, was persecuting you?

'My nemesis,' said the Dr, in a low voice, as if to himself. 'The Master Debater. Whom else could it be?'

'And *who*,' I said, drawing out the *oo* sound of the word and trying to slip the quietest-possible *m* at the end, such that it could be heard as either 'who' or 'whom' depending on the listener's state of mind, perhaps thereby heading-off the Dr's inevitable correction, something which was, frankly, starting to annoy me, '*is* this Master Debater?' I finished.

'He *is* a Time Gentleman,' said the Dr. 'Just as I am myself. He's from the Planet Garlicfree, as I am myself. But whereas I graduated the Gentlemen Facilities with a doctorate, he only managed a Masters. The bitterness of this failure soiled him inside.'

'Soiled?' asked Linn.

'Do I mean sullied? No matter. It messed him up, that's the important thing. Internally. I mean, internally-mentally, not internally-physically or anything like that. He was made bitter, resentful. He became prone to evil.'

'Prone to it?'

'Such a waste of his Time Gentlemanly talents. He and I. I and he. We were *best* friends at the College of Temporal Gentlemen. But now ...' The Dr shook his head and whistled disparagingly. 'Don't get me wrong. I love him like my brother. Or, perhaps like *a* brother. Well,' he said, rubbing his chin in the search for exact verbal precision, 'not a *brother* perhaps. But I certainly love him like a brother-in-law. Or, to be more precise, I love him like he was my brother's lawyer. Or my lawyer's brother. Who is also a lawyer, and not a very nice one.'

'You hate him.'

'Indeedy.'

'He certainly seems to be going to some lengths to persecute you,' I pointed out. 'Why might that be, do you think?'

'As to why,' said the Dr, 'I don't know. There *will* be a reason, I'm sure. Most people usually do have a reason for what they do, after all. The Master Debater will have some diabolic scheme in mind. But that's not to say I know what it is.'

'Is that the best you can do?'

'Master Debater!' cried the Dr, as if to the air. 'Oh, *wicked* Master Debater! *Why* must you tarry in the ways of ultimate wicked evility?' He raised his right fist to a point a little way in front of his face, and then rotated it slowly, as if examining it from every angle for the intrinsic interest of its knuckles.

'Can he ...' I asked, looking around me but seeing nothing, 'can he, you know. Can he *hear* you?'

The Dr looked crossly at me. 'Of course not. He's splashing around in the icy waters of the North Atlantic right now. How could he possibly hear what I'm saying inside my own TARDY in tempo-spacey travel in the vacuum of deep space?'

'I don't know,' I said, a little sulkily. 'I thought maybe ... I don't *know*.'

'What?'

'I thought maybe he was eavesdropping. You know, electronically. And that was why you suddenly addressed him. *I* don't know how your TARDY machines work, now, do I? And anyway, what was I *supposed* to think? Why *were* you talking to him if he can't even hear you?'

'I was being dramatic!' exclaimed the Dr, in an infuriated tone. 'I was trying to capture a little of the quasi-operatic excitement incipiently present in the situation. I don't know why I bother sometimes, honestly.'

'Well there's no need to be like that,' I said, hurt, to be honest, by the Dr's tone.

'Will you two stop it?' said Linn. 'We've got our next mission to consider.'

'Ah!' said the Dr. 'Yes. Gather round, assistants. Gather round.'

Linn stepped smartly to stand next to the Dr. I tried to do the same, but caught my knee on the edge of the central console in my haste. This was very painful. I yelped and doubled over, trying simultaneously to grab my knee and to keep my balance. I failed in both respects, and instead slammed my forehead against the console. This was also very painful.

After some effort I was able to pull myself upright. I could see stars. This was because the Dr, oblivious to my pratfalling, had pulled up a viewscreen schematic of the area of space through which we were travelling.

'Our next mission,' he was saying. 'Hell. We must avert a terrible dynastic squabble. Apparently a single stick-back-plastic apostrophe, inserted onto an official sign in exactly the right place, should do it.'

'What about this Stavros fellow?' Linn was saying. 'I don't like the sound of this Time Gentleman Violator.'

'Ow,' I said, rubbing my forehead. 'Ow, ow, *ouch.*'

'It's a nasty piece of work,' the Dr agreed. 'It's designed to destroy a Time Gentleman's braintide.'

'Braintide?' Linn asked.

'The sum total of his brainwaves.'

'Ah!' said Linn, in an *I see!* tone of voice.

'Ah!' I said in a *my-skull-really-hurts-I-mean-I-don't-want-to-alarm-anybody-but-I-just-may-actually-have*-dislocated-*my-knee* tone of voice.

'If Stavros, or one of his Garleks, aimed that weapon at my brain' — the Dr patted his own chest— 'it would be curtains for me. Those little velvet curtains about a foot tall that are drawn across the slot at the crematorium through which the coffin disappears. Those sorts of curtains.'

'I thought you said your brain,' I said, cross on account of my hurty head. 'Why were you tapping your chest?'

'That's where my brain is located,' the Dr said.

'So where is your heart?'

'Are.'

'Up *where*?'

'No – are – where *are* your hearts. I have two.' He tapped his head. 'One on the *left* and one on the *right* side of my head. It's always seemed to me an arrangement infinitely to be preferred. Or, perhaps not infinitely, but. You know what I mean.'

Chapter Eight

THE DOOM OF THE HELL-MET WOMAN

Finally, after what seemed like a very long-drawn-out journey, the TARDY rematerialised. 'We've arrived!' announced the Dr, somewhat superfluously. 'Here we are.'

'And this is the location of our mission?' Linn asked.

'Oh yes.'

'So where are we, exactly?'

'According to my screen here,' said the Dr, 'we're on a planet called, um.'

'Um?' I said.

'The Planet Um is in the Hesitant System,' Linn explained, in a superior voice, 'orbiting the Star Sch.'

'No, not um,' said the Dr. 'That was me pausing, trying to read the iddly-bittly typeface on this ... Hell. That's what it's called.'

'Hell,' I said. 'That doesn't bode well.'

'Well,' said the Dr, airily. 'I wouldn't read too much into that. It might be that Hell means something very *pleasant* and *inoffensive* in the local language. Something like, I don't know, Chicken Korma. Or Eiderdown. Or something.'

'Never mind all this chatter,' said Linn, impatiently. 'Let's sort out this mission. It's placing an apostrophe on an official sign, I think you said. Let's go *do* it! Let's *place* that apostrophe!'

The Dr was peering carefully at the screen. His brow had furrowed. 'Ah,' he said. 'Hmm. Yes ... well, *that* could prove a little tricky. Nope, we can't leave the TARDY. I'm afraid.'

'Why can't we leave the TARDY?' Linn asked.

'Well let me see if I can explain,' said the Dr, running a very unspringy and indeed bone-based hand through his springy, boneless hair. 'On Earth, where you come from ...' He paused.

'I know I come from Earth,' I said.

'Yes, yes. Don't interrupt me. I get distracted. Earth – on Earth, where *you*, Prose, originated – on Earth there is a substance known to scientists as *oxygen*. It's in the air.'

'This,' said Linn, speaking for the both of us, 'we know.'

'Well, *this* world, this planet Hell, has – well, to put it in technical scientific language, it has *no* oxygen in the air.'

'I see.'

'You don't sound surprised?'

'I'm not,' I said. 'I mean, I'm assuming it's pretty rare that you land on a world with precisely human-breathable air. As I understand it, the oxygen levels even on Earth have fluctuated quite considerably over the last forty thousand years. In the rest of the cosmos – well I'd guess that a million forms of life have evolved breathing everything from argon to zeon. Assuming zeon is a gas. Or am I thinking of neon? Anyway, anyway, the *point* is,

I'd assume that perhaps one in a trillion planets have atmospheres breathable by creatures such as us.'

'Well,' said the Dr, 'Hmm. It's. Actually it's quite complicated.'

'Is it? How?'

The Dr tapped at the monitor and brought up a visual representation of the world outside the TARDY. The scene displayed was of rolling hills covered in green grass, a pale blue sky, a bright yellow sun. It looked inviting. I mean, apart from the fact that the hills were rolling. I don't, incidentally, use *rolling* as a merely metaphoric or conventionalised description of the hills. These hills were literally rolling. Some hidden geologic force was slowly rotating them like colossal, green horizontal kebabs. They were grassy all over, though; and there were cows and even little rabbits visible upon them, who didn't seem too bothered by being dipped under the earth for long minutes. When they popped up again, they were still happily munching the grass. I assumed that their feet, or hooves, were adapted so as to be able to cling to the turf whilst it was upended. But I was unable to check my theory, because the Dr refused to open the door.

'I can't open the door,' he said, again.

'It looks very pleasant outside,' I pointed out.

'You two, you're not, you aren't *paying attention* to what I say,' he complained. 'There's no *oxygen*. Right? Step through that door and you'll choke.'

'Well alright,' said Linn, in a matter-of-fact tone of voice. 'I'm assuming you have breathing apparatus? For all the occasions when you visit planets that don't happen to have the precise and delicate combination of gases we're accustomed to on Earth? Isn't that standard Time Gentlemen gear?'

At this the Dr looked shifty. He shifted his eyes from side to side, and shifted his weight from foot to foot. He shifted his scarf, flicking it from over his left shoulder to over his right. I think you take the point that he was shifty.

'We don't usually have much call for breathing apparatus,' he said.

'Not much *call* for it? Are you *serious*?' asked Linn, incredulous.

My credulity was also in. 'It can't be the case,' I objected, 'that you *always just happen* to visit planets with breathable atmospheres?'

'Pretty much,' he said. Then he mumbled something, and looked away.

'And there's nothing—' Linn pressed, 'nothing in this entire TARDY, that would help us? Not so much as a gas-mask? Not even a *snorkel*?'

The Dr shrugged his shoulders. He wasn't meeting our eyes.

'I simply can't believe,' Linn continued, 'that there is not, in this entire spaceship, a *single piece* of breathing gear.'

'I'll go and have a look,' muttered the Dr, looking unhappy. 'There might be something in one of the ... you know. In one of the. Other rooms.' With this he slipped through a door and hurried away into the inner labyrinth of the TARDY.

'*Don't* just go for a little lie-down,' Linn called after

him. 'You go find us some breathing equipment, you hear? You *hear*, Doctor?'

There was no answer.

'Doctor?' she called again. 'Have you gone off to have a little lie-down somewhere? *Don't* you have a little lie-down! You fetch us some equipment, so we can go exploring on this world and sort out the apostrophe business on this planet! Do you *hear*?'

Nothing.

'Doctor?' screeched Linn. 'We're doing this for your benefit you know! Neither of *us* wants to go gallivanting about this strange planet. We're trying to help *you*!' She waited, with her ear to the door. 'You *have* gone to have a little lie down, haven't you!' she called.

'I think he may, actually,' I offered, 'indeed have gone for a little lie down.'

'Curse him,' said Linn without vehemence. 'Do you think we should try and winkle him out of whichever room he's run off to?'

'There are hundreds of rooms back there,' I pointed out. 'He could be in any of them. We'd be searching through them for hours and hours. Best let him have his lie down. He'll come back through when he wakes up. It might even recharge his batteries.'

'It's a—most—provoking—thing ...' Linn said, shaking her head.

'He certainly seems to like his little naps,' I agreed.

*

Linn was despondent for a few moments, and then she rallied herself. 'Hey! We don't need *him*. D'you know what I think? There's bound to be all the equipment we need right here, in the control centre. I mean, this is where you'd leave it, don't you think? If you needed it?'

'I suppose so,' I agreed.

Linn went over to the central control panel and opened a little door in its side. 'Aha! First place I look!' she exclaimed, delighted. She reached in and pulled out a helmet. It looked a little like a deep-sea-diver's helmet: a metal globe a little larger than an average adult human head, with a small glass screen in the front. 'I knew it!' she declared, sounding very pleased with herself. 'I knew there'd be something!'

'Will it fit?' I asked.

'It's *exactly* the right size. I wonder if it comes with, you know, oxygen tanks and such?'

'According,' I observed, reading from the side of the helmet, 'to this little plaque on the side it's all integrated into the device. Self contained air supply, water and even food. *Nutrition Pap Brand three-five-one-one*, apparently. *Your Time Gentleman Breathing and Life Support Equipment is Guaranteed for One Thousand Years*. Sounds just the ticket.'

'Doesn't it just?' she agreed. She reached back inside the cupboard and pulled out an identical-looking helmet. 'Here you go – one for you too.'

'You don't think,' I said, hesitantly, 'that the thousand-year guarantee has *expired*, or anything?'

'Nonsense,' she returned. 'They look positively *brand* new.'

I peered at the helmet in my hands. It was certainly a gleaming item, undusty and unscuffed. 'I suppose you're right.'

'Right,' said Linn, in a matter-of-fact voice. 'This is what I suggest. We put these on. We pop outside, have a look around, and hopefully work out what needs to be done to straighten the timeline here — find that sign, insert the apostrophe. It'll be good practice for me, and we can sort it all out before the Doctor even wakes up from his afternoon nap.'

'If you're sure that's a good idea—'

'Of course I am! Can you imagine his face when we come back? *Look Doctor, we sorted it all out whilst you were napping*! Ha-ha!'

'Well,' I said, uncertainly. 'OK.' I lifted up my helmet ready to put it on. Linn did the same.

Then something peculiar happened. In the split-second before I dropped the helmet over my cranium, Linn disappeared.

One minute she was there, and the next she had vanished. Completely vanished! I opened my mouth to shout in surprise, but my fingers at that precise moment let go of the helmet to drop it onto my shoulders. I barely had time to cry out.

Then everything went black.

The next thing I knew was an enormous crash and an earthquake-like shudder that knocked me from my feet. I'd like you to imagine — if you'll indulge me — a large warehouse built of reinforced steel girders and iron cladding, with a huge metal domed roof; and that this warehouse had then, somehow, been elevated six feet above the ground, suspended there, and then *dropped* onto a concrete or stone ground. That was the nature of the ear-splitting clatter that greeted me. It almost burst my ears. The reverberations from the collision echoed and re-echoed.

I picked myself up and looked about me. I had somehow been transported into a huge enclosed space, some kind of circular barn or hangar, lit by a dim window very high up in an enormous curving wall. The floor stretched thousands of yards away from me in every direction. A huge duct, wide enough for me to climb inside had I been so minded, dangled from the wall before me. I stared at this huge structure. It ended in a bizarre truck-sized sculpture in black rubber. It looked as though it might fit inside a giant's mouth as his gum-shield.

I turned slowly to examine my new surroundings. The roof was curved and groined like a giant version of the inside of the Dome of Saint Paul's. It towered so enormously over me that thin and wispy clouds were visible floating in at the zenith.

It took me only a moment to understand what had happened. Of course: the helmet was TARDY technology. It was, accordingly, *much* bigger on the inside than the out. I ran to the nearest portion of the wall – it was a brisk, ten minute jog away – and tried to slide my hands under the rim and lift the huge dome off me. But it was hopeless: It was like trying to – no: let me be precise, it was *exactly the same* as – trying to lift an entire eight-hundred-metre tall aircraft-hangar built of steel girders and iron claddings with my bare hands.

I couldn't even get my hands underneath the lip of the helmet. It was being pressed into the floor with a weight of many hundred thousand tonnes.

I sat back. This was bad. The space was chilly and I wasn't even wearing a sweater. Not even a *cardigan*.

The situation was dire.

'Help! Somebody!' I shouted. 'Doctor? Can you hear me? I'm trapped inside here! Lift up the helmet Doctor – take hold of this helmet and lift it up ...'

My words re-echoed. It was hopeless. I bashed my fist against the wall and it rebounded. The metal felt at least a metre thick: a huge and impenetrable barrier between myself and the outside world. And even if I could have communicated through this wall, the Dr was snoozing in some alcove deep inside the TARDY. And Linn – Linn must be trapped just like me.

I stepped back, and walked towards the middle of the dome again. Craning my neck I could see the window high above me – clearly I was looking at an inside view of the face-plate of the helmet: it might only be the size of a postcard on the outside, but it was a colossal expanse of glass on the in. For a while I idly speculated about climbing up to it – but it was many hundreds of meters above me and any climb would be a dangerous prospect indeed. And even if I could scale the sheer, curving wall, what would I do then? Wave at the Dr through the glass? But what if he didn't see me? He was still napping, somewhere in the bowels of the TARDY. If a spacecraft could be said to have bowels. Which, come to think of it, I rather doubted.

It was alright, I told myself. He would eventually wake up. Then he could come back through to the control room, and pick up the helmet. Though fantastically heavy on the *inside*, it weighed a matter of a few grams on the outside. The Dr would notice it lying on the floor, and lift it up to put it away – revealing me underneath it. All I had to do was wait out the intervening time.

It was a bore. But, I was unlikely to freeze to death in the space of a few hours. Even without a sweater.

I ran my fingers of my right hand up my left arm. The goosepimples there spelt out, in Braille (a script I had had to learn as part of my prose-tailor training) the message: HYPOTHERMIA CAN KILL IN MINUTES. I ignored this message. And, to be absolutely exact, because of the chance positioning of a large mole on my forearm next to a small crescent-shaped scar, it actually spelt out: HYPOTHERMIA CANNED KRILL IN MINUTES, which sounded more to me like a advertisement for a brand of tinned seafood. Which, by a strange chance, I have actually eaten. In a Krill restaurant upon my home world. But this is by the bye.

There was no immediate danger, then. But, insofar as I have always been an impatient fellow, I will confess that the prospect of several hours of shivering did not appeal to me. I decided that I had to think of a way out of this prison.

I turned myself about through three-hundred-and-sixty degrees to scan the whole inner surface of the thing. But I discovered that, whilst three-hundred-and-sixty degrees would have been enough to rotate the helmet through one entire turn on the outside, *inside* it barely covered a fifth of the perimeter on the inside. I turned and turned and turned until I was dizzy, and eventually I was again looking at the giant hose.

It took me a moment to stop feeling nauseous.

No more turning about, I decided.

The thing to do, clearly, was to take a closer look at this hose. From a distance its purpose seemed clear: it would feed oxygen into the mouth of anybody wearing the helmet. Of course, on the inside it was much too large to fit into any actual mouth. But I wondered if it would be possible to – for instance – climb inside it, work my way up the tube and perhaps find some egress to the outside world? It was a long shot, I knew; but I couldn't think what else to do.

As I walked towards it, the oddly pronged and curved shape of the thing grew larger and larger, until it lost all resemblance to a mouthpiece and became nothing more than a vast ebon blob, suspended in space. It looked like something Henry Moore might have sculpted out of eight tonnes of partially chewed liquorice. Which is to say, it looked extremely unappealing.

Finally I arrived at the foot of the structure. It was connected to the wall, some thirty metres above me, via a tube large enough to run trains underneath the English Channel. In both directions. The mouthpiece itself hung perhaps five metres from the floor – maddeningly too high to reach, even if I stood on tip-toes. Even if I stood on tip-toes and jumped up. I tried doing this, standing on tip-toes and leaping up, four or five times before it occurred to me that the muscles *in my toes* might be less effective at propelling my entire bodyweight into the air than, you know, the muscles *in my legs*. So I stood on the flat of my feet and bent my legs and tried jumping again. I jumped higher this way, but it was still useless.

What to do?

What happened next surprised me. A rope dropped from the open mouth of the huge rubber object above me. It trailed down like the first tendril of water from a giant black rubber bath-tap, silvery and glinting.

A moment later a figure came shinning down the rope – the figure, in point of fact, of a beautiful young female. She was dressed in a silvery top that was large enough to cover her upper body; and also in tiny green shorts that seemed to be made of some silky material which were quite inadequate to cover her lower body. When I say 'shorts', I could perhaps qualify the phrase and note that they were, in point of fact, knickers. As I later discovered. Her legs were long, lithe, lovely, and possessed several other alliteratively legsy 'l' qualities. They were wrapped tightly about the rope. She slithered down and came to a halt standing upon the floor facing me. For a while she did nothing but blink in the light. Then she said 'Why didn't you wake me up?'

This was a puzzler.

I said: 'I'm sorry, I didn't know I was supposed to.' That looks a bit ridiculous written down, I know. It sounded pretty ridiculous coming out of my mouth. But when a beautiful woman abseils down a silver rope in her knickers from the cavernous entrance to a fifty-metre-wide rubber mouthpiece suspended five metres in the air and demands to know why you didn't wake her up, it's hard to think of anything to say that wouldn't sound ridiculous. In fact, ridiculousness-sounding was the appropriate response, I feel.

'I can't *believe* I slept through it!' she cried in rank

frustration. 'Whom was it who lifted the helmet? Was it you?'

'It— I— er, yes.'

Her next question was: 'whom are you?' But before I could answer her eyes left me and stared at the cavernous space in which we were both standing. Her jaw fell, leaving her mouth completely open in astonishment. She gawped as if seeing her environment for the first time. 'It's so huge!' she gasped. 'Oh it's been so *long* since I saw it! So very long! I had forgotten – no matter how many times I felt my way around the perimeter with my fingers'-ends, it's not the same as actually *seeing* it like this. It's *astounding*!'

'Who *are* you?' I asked. I was ravished by her beauty. Her beauty was like an anchor, fixing me to that spot. She, in other words, was a ravish-anchor.

'It's *so* good to see another living being!' she cried, throwing her arms around me. 'It's been *so long* ...'

'Nice to meet you too,' I said, politely, in a squeaky voice. I could feel the soft and lovely warmth of her body in close proximity to mine. It had been a very long time since any woman, of whatever physical disposition (let alone one as beautiful as this one) had been in close proximity to me. Or middling proximity. Or far proximity, come to that. I was gobsmacked.

'Forgive me for my rudeness,' she said, stepping back and facing me squarely. 'And allow me to introduce myself. I am Lexanco, daughter of Panzpipl, from the planet Tapov. I am from the country of Lithe.'

'I am delighted to meet you, Lexanco,' I said. 'From the planet of ...?'

'Tapov.'

'I see. You are not human, then?'

'I am Lither.'

'I'm delighted to make your acquaintance,' I said. 'My name is Prose Tailor. I'm a tailor of prose – a human, from the twenty-third century. Might I ask about how you came to be here? This,' I added, gesturing to the relevant area, 'is my helmet.'

She looked amazed.

'Surely not!' she cried. 'How can it be *yours*? You seem so young! For I have been here for many years – too many years to count easily upon the fingers of my hands and my feet.'

'More than twenty years?' I gasped.

'More than thirty-one years,' she corrected. When I looked a little startled, she added: 'I am not human, after all.'

I glanced at her hands – each of which contained exactly five digits – and boggled briefly. But, I reflected, the ways of alienkind are generally strange. And in all other respects this figure was gorgeously and alluringly feminine. Now, I would like to describe her to you (I am, after all, a tailor of prose) but I'm afeared that my words would be inadequate – that they would merely skate over her figure; that they could not stay abreast of her breasts, would pip her hips, that I would, to put it in plain words, be telling lies about her eyes, being unfair to her hair. For my words could never capture the rapture of her stature. Which wasn't flature. I mean, flat. I mean it was *curvy*. The truth of the matter is that her figure was in *all respects* shapely.

I seem to be losing the thread a little.

Let me put this in as simple a manner as I can: I fell instantly in love with Miss Lexanco. Have you heard the phrase *love at first sight*? Have you ever experienced *love at first sight*? – or, I should say, have you ever experienced *sight*? Because until you have fallen in love at first sight you don't know what sight, in its fullest possibility, is. Unless you have fallen in love yourself then you can have no sense as to how I felt, at that moment, inside that aircraft-hangar-sized helmet, standing before that gorgeous, curvaceous and twenty-one-toed woman.

'You are staring,' she observed.

'I— I— apologise,' I stammered. 'It's just that I have never before seen so beautiful a woman!'

'How old are you?' she asked.

'Twenty-nine.'

'Then you and I have something in common,' she said, smiling kindly. 'For as I stand here before you, I can comment that I have never seen so handsome a man. At least not for the same period of time to which you alluded.'

'You've never seen a better looking man than me?' I asked in frank disbelief.

'Not in the last twenty-nine years at any rate.'

'But you've been inside this helmet for ... oh I see what you mean.' I was momentarily a little discouraged; but then the enormity of Lexanco's fate finally sank in. *Three decades* alone inside a gigantic helmet! It was beyond belief. It was *so far* beyond belief that it circled the planet of incredulity and arrived at the back of the head of the same belief of which it was beyond. I mean that I believed her. You see? That was the point of my metaphor.

'Three decades inside this prison?' I gasped. 'Without a single other sentient creature to keep you company? How terrible!'

'Indeed.'

My chivalrous instincts were aroused. I was, as it happens, aroused in other ways too, but let me not dwell upon those in what is, after all, a memoir designed for family reading. 'I shall rescue you!' I cried.

'Thank you,' she said. 'How?'

'Well—' I said. 'In a couple of hours I'm pretty sure that somebody outside will lift this helmet up.'

'You're *pretty* sure?'

'Pretty sure, yes.'

'It doesn't – forgive me for saying this – it doesn't sound like a *plan*, exactly. More a sort-of wait-and-hope strategy.'

My chivalrous instincts, formerly aroused, were now piqued. 'In that case,' I said, boldly, 'I shall rescue you straight away! We need not wait on the vagaries of fate. We shall make our way out of this prison without delay.'

'I am impressed,' she said. 'What will you do?'

I had no idea. To give myself time to think I asked. 'How have you survived for so long in here? Is your race of aliens one that has no need for sustenance?'

'On the contrary, I must eat all the time. My race of aliens, dear Prose, is not so very different to humanity. In my former travels I encountered humans many times, and I am very familiar with them. My people and yours are close enough genetically to permit friendship, marriage and even divorce.'

'So,' I said, trying to swing my arms in an insouciant manner and thereby express my eminent suitability for a session of experimental interbreeding, should she wish to test the possibility. 'So how did you manage to survive for thirty-two years inside this helmet? What did you eat?'

'I ate pap. There is a supply – it can be accessed by climbing up the mouthpiece tube. There is water there too.'

'Enough for thirty-two years?'

'Yes indeed. The portions, you see, are considerably magnified. The food is coarse and without flavour, but it contains enough nutrient to maintain life.'

'It doesn't sound very pleasant.'

'It is not. But it is preferable to the alternative.'

'What's the alternative? Some sort of food even worse-tasting? You know, like, like,' I couldn't for a moment recall the phrase I wanted, and then it came to me: ' – like airline food, ha-ha?'

'When I said preferable to the alternative,' she replied in her flat, slightly puzzled tones, 'I meant that the alternative would be death by starvation.'

'Oh,' I said.

There was a silence.

'Still,' I said. 'I'm terribly impressed that you managed to get up into the mouthpiece at all. *Terribly* impressed.'

'I unthreaded my trousers,' she explained, in her level voice, 'and wound the twine into a rope, and this I used to get up to the opening of the mouthpiece. Of course this has had the consequence of leaving my legs bare, and of forcing me to walk around in nothing but my knickers for three decades. But, once again, I preferred that to the alternative.'

I too preferred her walking around in only her knickers to the alternative. That sentence holds, actually, for pretty much any alternative you might care to name. My being crowned King of Norway, for instance. A lifetime's supply of chocolate headwear. A new cure for Chronic Bat Syndrome. Whatever alternative you can think of, I can assert that I would prefer watching Lexanco walking around in nothing but her knickers to it. In fact – and I've given this matter some considerable thought – the only alternative I can be sure I *would* prefer to watching Lexanco walking around in nothing but her knickers, would be the alternative in which I watched Lexanco walking around in nothing *not even* her knickers. But that wasn't on the cards. At least not immediately.

I decided, as tactfully as I could, not to try and put into words the thoughts expressed in that last paragraph, even though they all passed rapidly through my mind at that juncture. Instead I limited myself to saying: 'quite'.

'It has been a lonely time,' she said.

'I can imagine,' I said. 'And how did you come to be marooned here inside this helmet in the first place?' I asked.

'It is a long story,' she said. 'I was an assistant-stroke-companion to The Dentist.'

'To who?'

'To whom?'

'I asked *you* that.'

'I am not asking, but correcting. You said *to who?*, when the correct formulation must be *to whom?*'

But of course she had absorbed the passion for correct grammar and syntax from the Time Gentleman she had been accompanying. 'Whom,' I tried, 'is The Dentist?'

'No,' she said, 'in this case the correct formulation is *who is The Dentist?*'

'I'm terribly sorry,' I said. 'It's a poor thing for a prose tailor to confess, but I have to admit that I've never been very good on the difference between who and whom.'

Her eyes widened in shock, and I felt a sudden sickness in my stomach – for the fear had come abruptly upon me that I had alienated this beautiful creature. I'm ashamed to say that I panicked a little. More than a little. Alright, I panicked abjectly. 'Not,' I hurriedly added, 'but that I wouldn't be eager to learn the difference, from a teacher as expert and, um, alluring as yourself. You could certainly teach me the difference between *who* and *whom* – or between the two states of any nips you like. *Nouns*, I mean nouns. Nouns, not, ha! Ha-ha! Ha! Stupid of me. Embarrassing! I mean that sort of slip of the thong – of the *tongue*, the tongue, the tongue *tongue*. *That* kind of slip. Tongue. *Slippery tongue!*' I tried to calm myself. I was speaking much too rapidly. And a little loudly too. Some part of my consciousness was trying to blot out the fact that I had, only minutes after meeting her, yelled 'slippery tongue!' directly into the face of the most beautiful woman I had ever seen. I am, I concede happily, no expert on the business of chatting-up beautiful women; but I'm prepared to bet any amount of money that walking up to a woman you barely know and shouting 'slippery tongue!' in her face is not likely to persuade her to go home with you and crack open the bottle of baby oil. If I became fully aware of what I had just done I might well literally expire with embarrassment. I had to push on, not to lose my momentum, to try and salvage the situation. I took a deep breath, and decided not to say anything else.

She looked coolly at me for a moment. Then she said: 'Sir Tailor: if you can free me from this monstrous helmet, which has been my prison for so many years, I promise to teach you anything you ask.'

'Anything?'

'Anything.'

'Just to clarify, so as I understand. Anything?'

'Indeed.'

'Well, that's a very generous offer that y— *anything*?'

'It has been so long!' she cried in despair, balling up her fists and tapping at her own temples, a gesture I assumed was made to indicate her frustration. 'Trapped, alone, in darkness, eating pap! I waited – I waited – thinking, as you first said, that *somebody* would be sure to lift the helmet up and release me. Somebody! But *did* they? *Did they*? No! For a day and a night I sat in the middle of the chamber here, sitting cross-legged, until thirst and hunger forced me to explore the mouthpiece.'

'Ah, yes,' I said, seizing on this as a topic of conversation that would steer me free from the morass of embarrassment into which I had, against my better judgment, been striving to bury it. 'You were explaining how you got up there. You said you unpicked the threads of your silver trousers, and wove them together again as a rope. What then?'

'I used the buckles from my stylish patent-pretending-leather shoes as a grapple.'

'Your patent what?' I asked.

'Mock leather,' she said.

I was so pathetically eager to please her, so desperate to impress her with my openness, that I took her at her word without a second thought. I should have had that second thought, so as to prevent myself from making a fool of myself; but my brain was galloping on heat. 'Leather!' I said, in a scornful voice. 'It's rubbish, isn't it? All tough and – and *leathery*.' This didn't seem to me to be mockery enough, so I added in whiny voice, flapping my hands about for comic effect: 'oo I'm leather, look at me aren't I *versatile*,' before resuming in my normal voice, 'well *no* you're *not* actually, you're just *skin*, not even *living* skin, just *dead* skin, and *that's* the same thing that gets sucked up in my vacuum cleaner when I do the *hoovering*. Leather? Don't make me laugh.'

I stopped.

'I meant,' said Lexanco, 'not that *you should* mock leather, but that *they are* mock leather. The shoes.'

I thought about this.

'I see,' I said. Then I said. 'Yes, that makes more sense. I feel a little foolish.'

'So,' she said, neutrally.

I looked down at her bare feet. 'So, where are they now? Your shoes?'

'In my den.'

'You have a den, then?'

'Inside the mouthpiece. I use the shoes as all purpose utensils. Cups, scoops, containers, gloves. They have worn surprisingly well, really. I clambered up inside there and felt my way along the tunnel. There is a toggle just on the inside. It's designed, I suppose, to be operated by a tongue; it releases gushes of water, or pellets of food. The first time I tried it I was almost flushed from the tube! But at least I could satisfy my thirst from the residue clinging to the inside of the container. Then I ate some food. I crawled further into the mouthpiece to explore. It was dark, and the rubber was relatively soft underneath my knees and hands – much more so than the hard floor of the main chamber. I was exhausted, and fell asleep. The next thing I knew I was being thrown about, bounced from rubber wall to rubber wall.'

'The helmet had been picked up?'

She nodded, grimly. I grinned noddingly. This was an inappropriate reaction to her expression of gloominess, of course, but I seemed to have lost control of my face. Some part of me was still trying to ingratiate myself with her. 'Somebody – I know not whom – had picked up the helmet. And because I was inside the mouthpiece, rather than just standing on the floor, I was picked up too. The helmet was plunged into some dark space – perhaps the very cupboard from which you plucked it, so many years later.'

'I don't understand – how could your companion abandon you? You said you were with a dentist?'

'Not a. The. *The* Dentist – a Time Gentleman of *great* distinction.'

'What a coincidence! I too am the assistant-stroke-companion of a Time Gentleman! Mine is called The Doctor. And one thing of which I am sure is that he will not abandon me here, inside this helmet. How did your Dentist come to leave *you* here?'

'I do not know,' she said, sorrowfully. 'For many years I fretted and worried over this very question. Perhaps he merely forgot about me, for he *was* a trifle absent-minded. Perhaps some tragedy befell him and he was unable to rescue me. But as I lived on in the darkness, year after year, counting the passage of time by my periods of sleep, marked as notches in the soft material of the rubber wall of my den— well, to be truthful, darker suspicions began to crowd in upon my brain.'

'Darker suspicions?'

'That the Dentist had abandoned me deliberately, maliciously. That he, whom I had taken to be a force for Good in the cosmos, was actually a figure of evil.'

'But he was a Time Gentleman!' I objected. 'A guardian of virtue and honesty and order in the cosmos!'

'But how much do you *really* know of the Time Gentlemen?' she pressed. 'How much did *I* know? The Dentist arrived in this craft on my home world of Tapov, circling the star Thpops, and met me. Within a few hours I was whirled away, carried off in his marvellous machine to visit a succession of exotic and exciting worlds. He told me he was one of the good guys. I believed him. But *should* I have done?'

I was nonplussed by this, or I would have been if I had known precisely what nonplussed meant. Something to do with mathematics, I've always assumed.

'But tell me,' she asked, urgently, 'tell me of the world outside the helmet. Did you meet the Dentist?'

'No Dentist,' I said. 'Only the Doctor.'

'He is *your* Time Gentleman then? Please tell me!'

'That's right. I'm his assistant-stroke-companion.'

'Did your Doctor ever *talk* of The Dentist?'

'No.'

'Then perhaps,' she wailed, 'perhaps my Dentist is truly dead! Oh, my poor Dentist, perhaps I have maligned you! Perhaps you *tried* to help me – perhaps you lost your life in the very struggle to release me from this prison!'

'Wait a minute. Dentist? Come to think, he *did* mention a dentist,' I said. 'I've just remembered.'

'He did?'

'If we're talking about the same person,' I said. 'He talked not of The Dentist, but of That Tooth-Hurting Wino Git. It comes back to me now ... the Doctor once told me that he originally bought the TARDY off WhoBay, the hypernet sales site, from a Time Gentleman who happened to be in reduced circumstances. I'm trying to remember his exact words – some old codger who had sold everything else, even his own teeth, in the search for money to feed his drink-habit, and had finally sunk so low that he had to hock his own TARDY.'

'Ah,' said Lexanco.

For a while we both stood in silence.

'Well,' she said, in a small voice. 'It only goes to show. You should not trust some person who shows up on your home world and carries you off without so much as a by your leave.' She pondered some more. 'He *was* always a little tipsy, you know. Blundered about a fair bit. Double vision. Do you know, he once told me he had multiple hearts? I thought this was merely a physiological fact of

Time Gentleman anatomy, until I realised that he'd been looking at an internal scan of his own body with alcohol induced double-vision. He also told me he had two livers, four lungs and an invisible friend called Claudius.'

'He let you down.'

'He did. I assumed he would rescue me, and I was proved wrong.'

This made me think, uncomfortably, of the frequent evidence of unreliability that the Dr had demonstrated since I had known him. 'Well,' I said. 'Perhaps you are right. Perhaps we should do *more* than just wait around for the Doctor – for *my* Doctor, I mean – to lift the helmet up. Perhaps we'd better get ourselves out of this mess ourselves. Under our own steam. Rather than just depending, passively, upon the actions of others.'

'Yes,' she said. 'But how?'

And at that very moment, inspiration struck. 'I've got it!' I cried.

'What?'

'Look at the floor!'

She did so, and presented me with a view of the top of her head. It may seem silly to you, but the sight of that top of the head moved me almost as much as the sight of the rest of her body. Her hair was purple, the strands straight and parallel arcs, and the top of her cranium was marked with the tender and exquisite line of her parting. If you cannot conceive of a hair-parting as being tender, or exquisite, then you have never truly been in love. Perhaps it is the blend of vulnerability and intimacy that that slender sight of her scalp granted me, I don't know. Parting, a poet of Love once wrote, is a sweet sorrow –

what a foolish and ignorant thing to say! In this case it was a sweet *joy*. It took actual effort on my part not to leap forward and kiss the top of her head.

She looked up at me again. 'Why did you instruct me to look at the floor?'

'Don't you notice,' I said, my heart pounding, 'anything *odd* about it? You may have been padding around this space in your knickers for over three decades, but that was in the dark. Your helmet was inside a cupboard in the central console of the TARDY control room.'

'True.'

'Now it is resting on the floor of the TARDY itself. In the outside world it occupies a space no larger than a dinner-plate; but *inside* it takes up *acres* of space. Acres and hectares! Hectacres, probably.'

'And?'

'So the floor beneath us is the TARDY floor, except that it is magnified by a factor of – well, I can't calculate the factor. Certainly it's a *lot*. The floor I remember from the TARDY is perfectly flat and white. But when we look down the floor is bobbly.'

'Bobbly,' she said.

'Blobbly. As if paved with miniature cobbles. Trillions of them – I'm guessing those are the *actual molecules* of whatever substance the floor of the TARDY is composed. Being inside this helmet is like being inside a gigantic microscope.'

'I don't see how this helps us,' Lexanco said. Her brow was deliciously furrowed with noncomprehension. I wanted to kiss her forehead. In fact, to save time, I might as well admit that I wanted to kiss pretty much the whole of her, regardless of how long this process might take, and excepting only her big toes. I've always had something of a phobia about big toes. The rest of a woman's toes I'm fine with; they're even sweet, in a certain way of looking at things, all lined up in a row on the foot like that. But there's something a bit revolting about the big toe – knobbled and protuberant with that toenail like a chip of faded bakelite. Urgh! But I'm getting distracted.

'Don't you see?' I urged her. 'Every tiny imperfection or indentation in the floor will be *enormously magnified* inside the helmet. If we work our way around the rim of the helmet I feel sure we will find a gap eventually – something that might be only the tiniest of dint or scrape in the surface of the TARDY floor, but which will *inside here* be a trench large enough for us to climb out of.'

'You should not end your sentences with prepositions,' she observed.

'But *apart* from that, what do you think?'

'An excellent plan,' she said.

'There's no time to lose!' I cried, enormously excited. 'Let us start here and work our way clockwise around the rim. This helmet cannot be resting perfectly flat upon the floor – no floor is absolutely and perfectly flat, not on a molecular level! As soon as we find a gap we can escape.'

'It is a very good idea,' she said.

I did not add what I was truly thinking – that then, in the outside world, when her gratitude to me as her saviour temporarily overwhelmed her quite natural physical revulsion, I would be able to seize the chance for a cuddle. Perhaps two cuddles. Perhaps – and why not? – a whole series of cuddles. And what, I found myself wondering excitedly, is the collective noun for cuddles? A huddle of cuddles, perhaps? A gaggle of cuddles? Or, if the principle of naming collective nouns applies across the board (I mean that principle which chooses a word primarily by its randomness with respect to the thing being grouped: an unkindness of ravens, a metaphysics of chairs, an obliqueness of proctologists, that sort of thing), then perhaps a bacon-slicer of cuddles, or a venn-diagram of cuddles. Although, come to think of it, that last one isn't so random.

Anyway: the point is that I anticipated some form of affectionate reward for helping the beautiful woman – the girl of my dreams – to escape. My fantasising knew no bounds. Except, of course, the bounds of decency such as was consonant with the tenets of teatime family entertainment.

We set off at once, Lexanco leading the way and me following, keeping the wall of the helmet on our left. For the first ten minutes or so there was nothing: the base of the helmet sealed perfectly against the white, stippled surface of the floor. I began to wonder about the soundness of my reasoning: perhaps, I thought to myself, the TARDY floor was constructed from some space-age advanced material that kept itself perfectly flat. This thought was a distinct worry to me.

'What did you do on your homeworld of Tapov?' I asked, by way of making conversation.

'We danced,' Lexanco said, simply. 'Everything, our religion, culture and economy, is entirely based about the continual performance of the sacred dance. Tap dancing, from which our world gets its name, is one key component; but there are many other forms of the sacred dance. It has been my one consolation, in the many years of darkness, that I have been able to keep my body in shape and my thighs and buttocks trim by dancing the sacred dance.'

'Trim,' I said, nodding. 'Thighs. Hmm.'

'The point of the dance is to capture the sacred oneness of the cosmic principle of movement – stars and planets dance in their orbits, the very atoms out of which we are composed dance with quantum finesse and intricacy. By acting out the ritual with our own bodies, we connect with this core harmony of reality,'

'Buttocks,' I said. 'Yes. Trim. Hmm. Thighs.'

'I was apprenticed to a minor dance troop in my home town,' she reminisced. 'Every morning I practised the dance moves, moving arms and legs in carefully choreographed motions.'

'Trim,' I said.

To be honest my mind wasn't really *on* what she was saying.

'Wait!' she cried! I was snapped from my reverie. 'Look!'

'Where?'

'Oh Prose, you were right! Do you see?'

She was pointing at the base of the wall. There, in the fabric of the ground, was an indentation. It was shallow, no more than ten inches deep, but it was surely deep *enough* for the possibility of escape. Some scratch in the TARDY floor out there, *in here* grown to the size in which an adult might – just – wriggle free.

We both got down on all fours to peer more closely at this dent. 'Do you think it reaches all the way through to the outside?' I asked.

'There's only one way to find out,' she replied. 'To squeeze through. Shall I go first?'

'Be my breast,' I said.

'What?'

'*Guest*,' I said, rather too loudly. 'Be my guest. *Be* my, be-be-be— I said *guest*, definitely.'

She gave me a slightly puzzled look. 'Very well,' she said. 'I shall go through first, and you can follow.'

'Yes.'

She lay on her front and wriggled into the shallow indentation. Her head went under the base of the wall, but then she stopped. For some moments she lay there squirming and jiggling. It took me a moment to realise that she was calling to me. My mind was on something else. I can't, um, remember what exactly.

'Prose!' came her muffled voice, for perhaps the fourth time.

'Eh? What? Eh?' I said, startled. 'What! I *am* listening, honestly I am.'

'For the last time pull me *out* . . . I can't get through.'

I took her ankles in my hands and heaved her back. She emerged gasping. 'I can see the light,' she told me. 'The dent goes all the way under the helmet – all the way to the outside!'

'Fantastic!'

'Alas I cannot fit. My chest area is too ample to permit me to squeeze through. But you, Prose, are a man, completely lacking the more built-up or developed tissue around your ribcage. I feel sure you could get through.'

'Yes! I shall go at once!'

'And when you get to the outside of the helmet, you must promise to lift it up – carefully, straight up. Do you understand?'

'To free you. Of course.'

'I'll walk towards the centre of the helmet now,' she said. 'So that I am as central as possible when you lift the helmet. I don't want you to snag me as you pick the thing up!'

'I'll be careful,' I promised.

'Then we are but minutes away from freedom,' she cried, delightedly. 'For both of us!'

'No more delay,' I promised. I dropped straight down to my belly and wriggled like a tadpole. My head went under the wall, and my shoulders and chest followed, my arms by my side. I propelled myself by pushing with my feet, and by a generally wormy process of wriggling, inching forward. There was indeed light at the end of this shallow tunnel, as Lexanco had said: in fact the tunnel deepened as I passed into it, becoming broader and wider. Soon I was able to crawl. I passed underneath several dozen metres of helmet-wall above, the tunnel deepening all the time. Before long I was able to stand upright, and as soon as I could I was running for the light – a widening smile-shaped space of brightness directly ahead.

I leapt—

—and landed, tumbling and rolling, inside the control room of the TARDY itself. I was free!

I came to rest against the far wall of the machine, with

its curious pattern of inset circular alcoves, like gigantic exploded bubblewrap. 'Lexanco!' I cried. 'I'm free!'

I got to my feet, and there was the Dr. He was standing on the other side of the helmet in one of the doors.

'Where the bloody gecko did *you* come from?' he exclaimed. He had a look best described as 'startled'.

'Doctor! I was trapped inside the helmet!'

'What helmet?' said the Dr crossly. He had, evidently, just woken up from his nap. When I say *woken up*, I mean, was *in the middle of the slow and crotchety process of waking up*. He glowered blearily at me. 'What are you *talking* about?'

Meeting Lexanco had impressed itself so deeply upon me – love fountaining from my heart and filling my chest – that I couldn't think, for a moment, how I had gotten inside the helmet in the first place. 'Linn,' I said, and it came back to me. 'Linn and I decided to go outside and complete the mission whilst you were asleep.'

'But the air would be poison to you,' the Dr snapped, rubbing his left eye. 'I *told* you that.'

'We found two helmets inside the console there,' I explained. 'Breathing apparatus. We were going to put them on and ...'

'What are you *talking* about?' the Dr demanded, grouchily. '*What* helmets?'

He took a step forward.

Oh! That fatal, sleepy stride! How I wish he had stayed put – how I wish now he had carried on napping in whichever TARDY antechamber he had gone to. Or, at the very least, if only he had put his foot forward with less forcefulness; if he had tiptoed, or shuffled, rather than flinging his whole leg, like a championship Strider competing for the Striding Cup.

'Doctor! No!' I cried. Or do I only *imagine* that I cried out in this Bond-like fashion, in the nightmares that have haunted me since that day? Was I not, rather, struck dumb with the horror of what was happening right in front of me? Is this my subconscious prompting me to do something, to try and prevent the inevitable? Those nightmares! They plague me still!

The Dr's foot connected with the helmet, still lying on the floor in the middle of the control room. Inadvertently the Dr booted it. It flew, with the force of a well struck football, in a fast, straight line; skimming a little way above the floor. It struck the far wall, and bounced back, turning in the air; ricocheting off the central panel, and then rolling to a halt. It turned, and turned, and then clonked upright, rattling briefly on its rim before settling back on the floor.

'My toe!' cursed the Dr. 'Who left that damn thing there in the *middle* of the floor?'

But I was frozen to the spot in shock. 'No!' I gasped. 'No!' I rushed to the helmet and gingerly, very gingerly, I lifted it up. There was nothing – a nothing that for the briefest flickering instant fed my hopes (of course, it was absurd – but hope, as love, can subsist upon absurdity). But then, with the very slightest sensation of weight shifting inside the thing, she came tumbling out. She fell, collapsing through the open bottom of the helmet to slump onto the floor of the TARDY – full sized at last— but— dead, as dead as could be.

I howled.

'Will you keep it *down*?' hissed the Dr. 'Not only have I got a bit of a headache, *but* — now — I've *hurt* my *toe*.'

❊

How many times have I replayed, in my mind, Lexanco's last seconds of life? The beautiful Lexanco, the first woman I ever truly loved? Did she suffer? Did she even have time to register what was happening?

I imagine her walking dutifully towards the centre of the helmet, as we had agreed, looking forward to the moment when I would lift the device off her. But that never happened. Instead she must have seen the far wall of the helmet suddenly hurtling towards her. If the Dr, in the outside world, inadvertently kicked the helmet with enough force to propel it at, say, twenty miles an hour at the far wall, then *on the inside* it must have moved with a speed of *several thousand* miles an hour. Perhaps that solid wall of so many tonnes of metal, dashing towards her at the speed of a hyperbullet, had struck her before she had the chance to register what was happening. Perhaps she died in a blissful ignorance. I can only hope so.

❊

Still stunned, terrified that a like accident might happen to Linn, I tremblingly lifted the second helmet, to reveal her standing, looking cross, and saying 'you took your time ...' But once I saw that she was safe I could no longer hold myself up. I collapsed on the floor of the TARDY sobbing like a shower attachment. I mean, in case that this simile does not paint a clear picture in your mind, a shower attachment through which water is flowing. Luke-warm water, of course. Body-temperature water, in fact. I know people talk of 'crying hot tears', but that has never convinced me. It's not as if human tear ducts have the capacity to add heat to the saline fluid that passes along them. So: the point of the simile is to stress how many and forceful were my tears. Hence, shower attachment.

Anyway, I cried.

Chapter Ten

THE GENESIS, DEUTERONOMY
AND BOOK OF TOBIT OF
THE GARLEKS

It was a dark and stormy night on the planet of Skary. At the same time it was a bright and sunny day. That's the thing with planets: it's night and day *at the same time* on any given planet. Planets, with their offensive roundness, thumb their noses at the simple rule that *night follows day in chronological order*. There's a reason for that chronological order, you know. It helps keep the timeline straight. This is one of the reasons why Time Gentlemen hate planets.

The TARDY materialised at dusk. It assumed the shape of a Skaryish Police Megaphone: a tube not unlike an alpine horn, although roughly twice as large. The Dr, Linn and I emerged from the round open mouth of the horn: it was like stepping out of an ivory cavemouth.

The air outside was cool. In the distance the landscape retained some of its beauty: purple-coloured mountains serrated the horizon; dark blue trees, tall as church spires, waved and hushed in the evening breeze. The sky was plum. But nearer at hand was evidence that a large scale war was being fought. We were standing upon a plain of churned mud, with so many craters that it looked like a stretch of brown bubble wrap in which all the bubbles have been popped. The stumps of wrecked trees, like burnt down fuses, poked up here and there. Away to the left a broken tank was half buried in dirt: one of those old style tanks on which the tank-tracks went all the way around the body in a giant parallelogram. Either it had been blackened by fire, or else somebody had gone to a lot of trouble with a tin of black paint and a brush. I assumed the former explanation was the more likely.

'Well,' said the Dr, looking around himself. 'Here we are. The Planet Skary. The Skary Planet. A war has been being fought here . . .' He paused. 'Is that right? *Has been being*? It sounds a bit odd to me.'

'No, I mean yes.' I said. 'I think that's right.'

'Perhaps it should be *will have had been being*? I get my tenses mixed up sometimes.'

'It's to be expected,' said Linn, reassuringly. 'What with all the confusions of time travel and everything.'

'I suppose so. Anyway. Long war. Lo-oo-ong war. Between the Dhals and the Kababs. Over food. Specifically, over the correct way to *prepare* food.'

At this mention of food Linn scoffed. 'Nobody fights wars over such a thing!' she said, scoffish.

'Your scoff,' said the Dr, 'is misapplied. There are plenty of worlds in this galaxy where wars have been fought over much less. And actually the peoples here on Skary have a genuine disagreement. The Dhals think food should be a bland, healthy pap. The Kababs think food should be highly flavoured, dripping with saturated fat and terribly *terribly* bad for you. The Kababs also smoke.'

'The Dhals don't smoke, then?'

'Oh they do. But they smoke herbal cigarettes.'

'Are they better for you?'

'No. Worse. And foul-tasting. But, you know. They're herbal. Anyway, so, it's a radical clash of cultures. Centuries of war.'

'Remind me why we've come here?' Linn asked.

'To make one of the largest corrections to the grammar of cosmic history ever to have been attempted by any Time Gentlemen,' said the Dr proudly. 'To undo the *greatest* of evils. Come – the Kabab base is westward from here. Destiny calls us.' He put his head back and started striding purposefully over the wasted land. His left foot went into the mud and didn't come out, even though his right foot was already advancing its stride. Accordingly he went straight down, forward, face-first into the mud, like a fairground target hit with a pop gun.

Linn and I helped him to his feet. 'You need to take care,' I said. 'What with all this mud, you know.'

'I do,' the Dr agreed ruefully. He tried to wipe the mud from his face, but succeeded only in smearing it more thoroughly. 'Am I clean?' he said, looking up at us. 'I have a date with destiny. Don't want to meet destiny all grubby.'

'Clean,' I said, not wanting to discourage him. 'Ish.'

'Did you say Ish, or shh?' the Dr queried, a little querulously.

'I said ish.'

'You see, *clean—shh*, would mean that I should shut up about being clean,' the Dr said. 'Which would in turn imply that I was pretty dirty, actually.'

'Ish,' I repeated.

'Cleanish?'

'Clean*esque*,' I clarified. 'Quasiclean.'

'Cleanikins,' suggested Linn.

'Words,' said the Dr ruefully. 'When will somebody devise a less ambiguous mode of communication?'

I think we both assumed this was a rhetorical question, but after several seconds the Dr repeated it, adding 'eh? eh? do neither of you *know*?' and then concluding 'in the year thirty-one-forty-four in the Gala Galaxy. Do you know *nothing*, either of you?'

'Apparently not,' said Linn.

'Come on,' said the Dr. 'This evil catastrophe won't avert itself, you know.'

*

We picked our way carefully through the craters and over the mud until we reached a low concrete structure surrounded by trenches. There we were greeted by several uniformed men carrying rifles. Or perhaps it would be more specific to replace the word *greeted* with the word *grenaded*. The first soldier tossed a grenade, which exploded a little way behind us and threw us into a heap at the feet of the soldiery. 'Why did you do that?' the Dr snapped at the tossy fellow, crossly. 'There's no call for that sort of behaviour!'

'The grenade was by way of saying *how-do-you-do*,' said the man who had pitched the thing at us.

'Well,' said the Dr, pulling himself to his full height. 'This is my way of saying very well thank you.' He slipped his hand in his pocket and pulled out the Moronic Screwdriver. 'Hah!' he cried. 'Experience moronicity, you aggressive fellows!' With a flick of his thumb he angled the screwdriver at the soldiers. 'This will teach you to mess with the Doctor!'

There was a high-pitched whine. One of the soldiers seemed to cock his head. Not in the way that a person might cock a gun – which is to say, it's not that he reached round with his thumb and pulled his head sharply backwards with a resonant click. That would, evidently, be silly. Rather he tipped his head to one side.

'An interesting device,' I said to the Dr.

'Indeed,' he said. 'It focuses moronness into a coherent beam. I'll give them a minute or so, and then these guys should be easily moronic enough for us to slip past them. Look! See! It's working.'

'You know,' the soldier was saying, in a strange voice. 'Hmm, Intelligent Design, yes. *That's* a very sensible explanation of things ...'

'You fool,' came a voice from the left. An officer was stepping through a concrete doorway into the trench. 'He's moronicizing you. Quick! Guns out!'

The Dr span about to focus the ray on this newcomer; but he was too slow. A pistol shot rang out. The bullet struck the screwdriver on its shaft, and the little device pinged out of the Dr's hand to land in the pongy mud.

'Hey!' the Dr complained. 'You could have had my thumb off there!'

'Take them into custody,' the Kabab captain ordered. The soldiers surrounded us at once, guns at the ready, bayonets pointing in towards us. The soldier who had spoken was shaking his head as if trying to dislodge something.

'Take them to the Leader!' the captain cried.

❈

We were marched at gunpoint into the heart of the Kabab concrete complex. Though, now that I come to think of it, I had rarely been in such a heartless place. So 'the heart of the complex' is a bit of a misnomer. 'Core' maybe. We passed many military men marching in the opposite direction, Kabab soldiers marching onwards, marching as to war, with the cross expressions of men about to go into battle and maybe get killed focused on those marching on before.

'I'm assuming this isn't good,' Linn said to the Dr.

'Nonsense,' said the Dr, unconvincingly. 'It's all going splendidly to plan.'

'They've captured us! They have us at gunpoint!'

'Us, yes. But not the TARDY. This is why I landed it on the wasteland out there, and not inside this complex. To keep it safe.'

We emerged into a large chamber. A number of cast iron and riveted doors were set into the far wall. The TARDY, still in its Skaryish Police Megaphone shape, was sitting in one corner. The Dr put his face in his hand.

'That *yours*, is it?' the Kabab captain said. 'I thought so. My men found it in the middle of the battlefield, and brought it here. Good job they did, too: we're about to begin a massive bombardment of the Dhal positions. Your ... device ... would have been smashed to smithereens. Smithered to smashereens. All smashed and smithed.'

'There's been a misunderstanding ...' said the Dr,

stepping forward. A soldier's bayonet jabbed at his stomach, and he danced back again.

'Against the wall over there, *if* you please,' shouted the captain. 'The Leader is coming!'

We lined up against the far wall obediently. One of the iron doors opened with a clang. Or perhaps I mean clank. The air of expectation in the room was enormous. Enormous air. Expectationish.

A strange figure, seated in a motorised wheelchair, rolled through.

'Stavros!' said the Dr. 'The real original Stavros – in the flesh!'

And what flesh it was. This Stavros, wheeling now into the centre of the room, appeared to have been most hideously disfigured. Hair sprouted in hectic profusion from his head, from his nose and his ears. His cheeks and chin had been scraped clean of hair, but still bore witness to their essential hirsuteness with a prodigious spread of fat black dots. There was more hair in one of his eyebrows than on my entire head. His upper lip bore a moustache of such dense hirsuteness that, had it been detached from its facial location and nailed along the base of a door, would have functioned as an extremely effective draught excluder.

It's said that kissing a man without a moustache is like 'eating a hard-boiled egg without salt'. Not that I've ever understood that saying, to be honest. Nor indeed have I kissed any men, with or without moustaches. Unless you count kissing one's own reflection in the bathroom mirror for, you know. Practice. But, anyway, if we stick with that analogy, the egg-without-salt metaphor, then kissing

Stavros would be like eating a hard-boiled egg whilst also consuming the annual production of the entire Siberian salt-mining industry.

On second thoughts, that's probably an over-elaborate way of explaining that his moustache was extremely hairy.

But the most startling thing about Stavros was his *skin*: dark brown, leathery, wrinkled, it looked as if he had been baked in an oven for weeks. Like a conker.

Stavros wheeled himself into a central position in the middle of the room. Then he surveyed the small group gathered about him, placed a cigarette between his lips, lit it, inhaled deeply, and then he spoke: 'hello ever-a-body peeps.'

'Hail Stavros!' cried his followers in unison. 'Hello!'

'Is good,' said Stavros, stubbing out his quarter-smoked cigarette on the panel in front of him and immediately lighting another one. He nodded in our direction, his mighty moustache wobbling. 'Ooziss?'

'Prisoners,' repeated one of his followers. 'Prisoners, oh Greatest of Greeks. This one claims to be a Doctor.'

'My cousin Avraam, he's a Doctor,' said Stavros. 'Innit.'

'I'm not that sort of Doctor,' said the Dr, stiffly.

'Oh, oh-oh-oh, *Time* Gennleman, izzit?'

'Indeed.'

'Ah! Enemy alien. They are opposing every-a-thing I stand for, peeps, these time gennlemen. They wanna maintain all the linear order of history and such, and I wanna mash every-a-thin into a big *stew*.' He licked his lips, stubbed out his cigarette and lit another one.

'I pooh-pooh you *and* your stew!' defianted the Dr. Stavros looked at him impassively, as if this taunt meant nothing, and as if the word 'defiant' couldn't be used as a verb in that matter.

'And woziss?' he said, wheeling himself over to the alpine-horn-shaped TARDY.

'Leader!' barked the captain. 'This is the alien's time-travel device! It has disguised itself as some kind of police communicator, but there's no doubt as to its identity.'

'Very interesting,' said Stavros, 'innit. Lucky day. You and you, carry this thing downstairs to my kitchen, er, *lab*. I am gonna wanna examine this in more detail. Find out how it works, take it apart and put it back together innit. Then I can build my own time-a-travel machine, and send the my evil cyborgs through the complete range of time and space.'

The TARDY was on a wheeled platform of some kind, and Stavros' soldiers set about pushing it through a door and away.'

'Hmm,' said the Dr, watching his TARDY – our only hope of escape, and the key to Stavros's domination of the galaxy – being hauled out of sight. 'That's probably not, on balance, a positive development. Stavros has always hated the Time Gentlemen, and sought to undo everything that we have achieved. And now we have, inadvertently, given him the technological power to do just that.'

'Oops,' I said.

'Surely he can't be *that* bad,' said Linn. 'I mean, looking around us, this is all pretty rudimentary ... technologically speaking.'

'You need to understand the full story of Skaryan history,' said the Dr, sorrowfully. 'Once upon a time it was a planet very like Earth. Blue skies, green fields, worldwide satellite television coverage. Stavros Pastapopolos was a celebrity on this world – a celebrity chef on Skaryan television. Then this world was ravaged by global war, and in the aftermath two things mattered more than anything else: firstly control of the food resources, and secondly control of the mass media. Food for the body, and food for the brain. A power-elite seized power: nobody could oppose them because they combined a tight control over food distribution with a propaganda stranglehold over all TV channels. The Celebrity Chefs! *Les Chefs du Monde*!'

'That's not anything,' said Linn, confidently, 'that could ever happen on *my* home world.'

'Power was seized by a cabal of a dozen Celebrity Chefs,' said the Dr, picking up the narrative. 'And they ruled the world with an iron skillet. They brought misery to millions. Eventually the populace rose up and overthrew them ... they were all thrown into a giant copper braising pot and braised to kingdom come.'

'Is that how his skin came to be so disfigured? Is that the result of ... braising?' I asked.

'Actually, the reverse is true,' said the Dr. 'His skin was so leathery and tough that the braising had little effect upon him. He acquired his marmite-hued dermis as a result of severe ultraviolet burning, a function of the time Stavros had spent under the fierce sun of his native land, far to the south of here. It evidently enabled him to survive the copper pot, and finally to escape, to organise Kababian resistance to the Dhaliesque counter-revolution. But he has carried his seething resentment with him ...'

'You must-a-not *seethe* resentment, innit,' broke in Stavros. 'You gonna kill all its flavour. Resentment gotta *marinade*, OK? I marinaded my resentment for many many years, and I's ready now to pay the cosmos back. Bring in the first of my Garleks, innit!'

A second iron door clonked open, and a machine glided through. Glid through. Glidened. Came gliding through. The first Garlek I saw with my own eyes.

It was based, obviously, upon the garlic; but was robotized and metallic and terrifying beyond all imagining.

Picture if you will a whole head of garlic: the fat, slightly cardboardy stalk about which are clustered, in a pear-shaped lump, dozens of bulging cloves. Imagine such a structure reproduced eight-feet-tall in metal and plastic; the stalk bent over at the top to provide some form of telescopic sight. Now imagine this creation rolling effortlessly across the floor, swivelling what looked like the barrel of a gun from its midriff, and above all exuding a pungent, unmissable, choking, gagging stench ...

I coughed. Linn coughed. But Stavros seemed delighted with the reek of his creation.

'Stop!' he commanded, and the robot stopped. 'Ready to bring a little spice to the universe, innit,' he declared to the whole room.

'Spice? *Geno*spice more like,' exclaimed the Dr.

'No,' said Linn. 'No, I don't get that one at all.'

'Genocide,' said the Dr, in a lower voice. 'I meant.'

'Same difference,' said Stavros airily.

'You're a megalomaniac!' cried the Dr.

'Izza good Greek word,' Stavros agreed, with some satisfaction. 'Megalo, that's meaning *big*, and Mania is a-meaning *frenzy*. I like it.' He smiled broadly. Or I think he smiled. To be honest it was hard to see what was going on behind that moustache.

'Hail Stavros!' cried the soldiers.

'As I was saying,' Stavros said, wheeling his electric wheelchair in a little circle around the stationary robot. 'Garlic, or *Allium sativum*, izza vegetable closely related to the onion.' He pronounced the word with the emphasis on the final syllable. 'It don't grow in the wild, peeps, and was first cultivated in *Greece*. And not Turkey, as some blokes is arguing, that's simply a lie. Izza *Greek*, innit.'

'Yes Stavros!' cried his followers.

'And now it finds its ultimate form, ever-a-body peeps. Inside this robotic case is a genetically modified Kababster. I have used all my culinary and scientific genius, innit, to cross a living Kababster with a big old chunk of garlic.'

'You crossed a person with a piece of garlic?' Linn cried in horrified disbelief.

'Exactly, innit. You might say he's a half cove and a half clove.' Stavros seemed to find this very funny, and laughed a cough-y sort of laugh as he lit another cigarette. Nobody else laughed. 'Anyway, the Garlek is a new breed. Is got the intelligence of a man, and the ruthless bitterness of raw garlic. The universe will never be so bland again!'

'Hail Stavros!' cried the soldiers.

'I gotta twenty thousand of these babies sitting in a big hangar, innit' said Stavros. 'And I am passing out the order, ever-a-body, that all military and police duties are now gonna be handled by them! They in charge now! Well, *I'm* in charge of them, but they in charge of ever-a-thing *else*!'

'Hail Stavros,' the soldiers repeated, a little less enthusiastically.

'Don't worry, peeps,' said Stavros. 'You're not gonna be redundant, innit. The old Kababster army is gonna be absorbed into the greater Garlek peace-keeping forces. Sooner or later you all gonna get the treatment, get crossed with garlic and given your own cyborg unit to drive about.'

'Hail Stavros,' said the soldiers, weakly.

'I gonna show you how it goes with these prisoners here. Is nothing to be afraid of, innit.' He pressed a button on his control panel and the Garlek robot shuddered into life. 'Garlek, can you hear me, innit?'

The machine rasped a reply: *'AFFIRMATIVE!'* Its metallic voice sounded like nails being dragged down a blackboard.

'You see those prisoners over there?'

'AFFIRMATIVE!'

'What are you going to do, Stavros?' demanded the Dr. 'Kill us, in cold blood?'

'Nah,' said Stavros, stubbing out a cigarette and lighting another. 'My Garlek is gonna take you down to the lab, and I'm gonna turn you all into Garleks. Cross you with cloves, innit. Then you'll work for me.'

'Never!' said the Dr, defiantly.

'You won't get no say in the matter, innit,' snarled Stavros. 'Garlek?'

'AFFIRMATIVE!'

'Take 'em wayaway.'

The cyborg rolled towards us, its gun-stalk quivering.

❋

We were marched at Garlek-gunpoint out of the chamber and along a sloping downward corridor. Things were looking bleak.

But the Dr did not seem discouraged. Indeed, he ende-avoured to strike up a conversation with the creature.

'I must say I admire the sheen of your bodywork,' he said, chattily. 'On that, er, metal *skirt* you're wearing. These half-globes. How do you get them so polished-looking?'

'IT'S LAMINATE! IT'S *LAM-IN-ATE*!'

'Is it? I see. Very interesting. Although I wonder if it's altogether *manly* to be, you know – wearing a skirt?'

'A *SKIRT* MINE AINT!' responded the cyborg in outraged mechanical tones.

'I stand corrected. Clearly not a skirt. Evidently some-thing much more masculine. Now, I can see the purpose of that eye-stalk, and of that laser-beam weapon thing you got there. But what's the point of that whisk-like protuberance on the left? Is it for the stirring of eggs and suchlike?

'AFFIRMATIVE!'

'It's certainly a large one,' said the Dr, admiringly. 'I'm

sure you could stir three or even four eggs simultaneously with that protuberance.'

The Garlek shuddered, and screeched. 'EGG-STIRRING— *EIGHT*! *EGGS!-STIR!-RING!-EIGHT!*'

'As many as eight at one go?' asked the Dr. 'Really? How interesting. I'm sure you have several most delicious recipes for eggs. Your creator, after all, is the famous Stavros Pastapopolos.'

The conversation seemed to dry up for a bit.

'Cake mix?' the Dr tried. 'I mean, I suppose as well as whisking eggs you could whisk up some lovely cake mixture with that whisk?'

'AFFIRMATIVE!' barked the Garlek.

'Do you know my favourite bit of baking cakes?' the Dr asked. 'Licking the mixture off the whisk afterwards. Getting your tongue in between the metal wires of the whisk to lick off all the …'

This seemed to make the Garlek very cross indeed. 'LICKS TERMINATE!' it shrieked. 'LICKS *TER-MIN-ATE*!'

'Alright, keep your hair on,' said the Dr. 'I daresay Stavros doesn't permit people to lick the bowl, or the whisk, in *his* kitchen.'

'He's pretty mean, that Stavros,' Linn agreed. 'I mean to say. Wanting to turn us into hideous half-garlic monstrosities. That's pure *meanness*, I'd say.'

'*EXTRA* MEAN!' agreed the cyborg, with pride, adding at once 'WAIT!'

We had arrived at the top of a staircase, leading down into the bowels of the complex. 'So what do we do now?'

asked the Dr. 'I mean, I'm sure a staircase isn't going to stop you. I'm assuming that you're fitted with some kind of stair-floaty-uppy-downy device?'

'AFFIRMATIVE!'

'Is that fitted as standard, then? Or does that come as a fitted extra?'

'EXTRAS INNATE,' screeched the metal being, for some reason getting very excited, and quivering from side to side on its fat round base. 'EX-TRAS *INNATE*! *EX-TRAS INN-ATE*!'

'So in effect,' said the Dr, 'you can fly?'

'*DETERMINATE*!' the creature cried. '-edly' it added, and to prove its point it lifted from the floor and floated through the air.

It shepherded us down the stairs and into a cluttered laboratory; exactly the sort of space you might associate with an evil dictator with a penchant for unspeakable experimentation. There were benches cluttered with all sorts of test-tube-racks, microscopes, colanders, chopping boards and sabatier knives. There were large microwave ovens, and away at the back were a series of glass tanks lit with a sickly green light. Inside these strange and monstrous creatures slithered and slid. I had no desire to examine it too closely, and indeed I was not given the chance.

A second Garlek was standing to attention over by one of the benches, and the first Garlek marched us over to this.

'Well,' said the Dr. 'This is – this is not good.'

'Indeed not,' I agreed. 'What can we do?'

'Do?' came Stavros's voice. 'You can get transmuted

into Garleks, innit.' He wheeled out of the shadows and into the centre of the laboratory.

'How did you get down here so quickly?' the Dr demanded.

'I took the service elevator, innit,' said Stavros. 'You! Garlek number one!'

The Garlek that had escorted us flipped its egg-whisk up in salute.

'You can go, innit. Go back to the surface and co-ordinate an attack upon the Dhals. I want ever-a-one of them slottered, OK?'

'AFFIRMATIVE!' shrieked the Garlek. It wheeled about and scooted away, leaving us with the evil genius, the second Garlek, and a laboratory full of dangerous implements.

'Right,' said the Dr, eyeing Garlek number two nervously. 'So, here we are.'

'What I wanna know,' said Stavros, lighting up a cigarette, 'is what you *doing* here, innit.'

'Well, we were just passing through, you know ...' said the Dr, vaguely.

'Passing through?' asked Stavros.

'Yes.'

'On your way somewhere?'

'Exactly.'

'And *not*, I-dunno, sent here by the Council of Time Gennlemen to destroy my Garleks before they can dominate the galaxy, innit?'

'Oo no,' said the Dr, glancing nervously at Garlek number two. 'Nothing like that.'

'Cause, you see,' said Stavros, 'that would suggest to

me that my Garleks are destined to become the greatest threat the galaxy has ever seen. Innit.'

'We-e-ll,' said the Dr. 'I'm not sure I'd go quite that far—'

'It'd be pretty gratifying to me to think so,' said Stavros.

'Excuse me, Mr Stavros, sir?' put in Linn.

'Chef, innit,' said Stavros.

'Chef, yes. Excuse me, chef. I was just wondering. Why are you so dedicated to evil? I mean, why not give *good* a go? Couldn't your Garleks be just as effective as forces for good?'

'Good— is just another word for bland,' said Stavros, dismissively. 'You wanna boil all the bitterness out of my Garleks, do you? Nah. Now, enough chatting, innit. Time to turn you all into half-clove monstrosities, destroy your free will, fit you with cyborg exoskeletons and turn you loose upon the world filled with hate and the desire to destroy. Innit.'

'Or else?' asked the Dr.

'What you mean, or else? Or else I'll get my Garlek there to blast you with its death-gas of concentrated garlic-essence and *no* mistake. You die *nasty* that way, I assure you, innit.' He gestured towards the Garlek with his cigarette. 'You better do as I say,' he concluded.

The Dr glanced at the Garlek once again. 'Hold on a second,' he said.

He walked briskly up the death-cyborg. 'No, Doctor,' I cried out. 'What are you doing?'

'Don't fret Prosy,' he declared.

'But Doctor! It'll destroy you!'

But heedless of my warning the Dr was reaching out with his right hand to grasp the death-gun stalk of the Garlek. I couldn't watch: I closed my eyes.

I heard a single click.

I opened my eyes again just in time to see the Dr disappear into the Garlek. He had – somehow – pulled open the front of the casing of the device, and was now stepping literally inside it. He vanished.

'Hey!' Stavros was shouting. 'Hey! What's a-going on!' He was jabbing at his control panel with a leathery hand, trying to get the Garlek to respond. But nothing was happening.

Almost at once the Dr appeared again, stepping briskly out of the Garlek casing. In his hand was a pen-sized silver stalk: a Moronic Screwdriver.

'Your soldiers shot my last one of these to pieces,' he was saying. 'But luckily I always keep a spare in the drawer in there.'

'That's— that's— the TARDY?' Linn gasped.

'Of course. Don't you remember – Stavros here ordered his men to bring it down to the lab? He was going to experiment upon it.'

'But it was in the shape of a giant horn.'

'Well, it *was*. But up in the bunker, there, Stavvy issued an order turning over all army *and police* duties to his Garleks. We all heard him. And since he's dictator his words have the force of law. The metamorphosing software inside the TARDY responded by changing its outward appearance to conform with the new policing regime. I wasn't sure at first, but the more I looked the more convinced I became that this wasn't a real Garlek at all. My own ship! Ha! You weren't expecting *that*, were you, Stavros?'

It was evident that Stavros was infuriated. 'Tzatziki!' he swore. 'Spanakopita! I'll *get* you for this, Doctor, innit!'

'We'll see about that,' said the Dr, aiming the Moronic Screwdriver at the head of the evil dictator. 'A few minutes of this and he'll be too moronic to do anything evil at all. He'll be too busy working out how much drool to dribble to be concerned with grandiose plans for taking over the galaxy.'

'Why not just kill me?' Stavros demanded.

'Nonsense,' said the Dr. 'I don't kill people. That's not my style.'

'And yet you would put an end to the whole race of the Garleks,' said Stavros. 'Is that not murder?'

'Don't quibble ethics with me,' said the Dr, aiming the Moronic Screwdriver at the dictator's nutbrown forehead. 'No ethiquibbling from *you*, thank you very much.'

'My body is already ruined,' cried Stavros, flapping a leathery hand over his control panel. 'If you destroy my mind it will be tantamount to killing me! You might as well go the whole hog!'

'When I think of all the evil you have performed in your time . . .' said the Dr.

'Doctor,' said Linn, with a tone of unease in her voice.

' . . .and all the evil you are planning to perform . . .'

'Doctor, stop a mo,' Linn said.

I, too, could sense that something was wrong.

'Don't interrupt me, Linn,' said the Dr. 'I'm just getting to the bit where I harangue him for his evil.'

'Something's wrong, Doctor,' said Linn, looking around.

'She's right. Something's not right,' I agreed. 'I mean. She's not wrong, something's wrong. Here. What I'm trying to say, by way of agreeing with Linn, is that *she* is right to suggest that something is *wrong*.'

'What are you talking about?'

'Stavros seems to have lost his Greek accent,' I observed.

'Has he?'

I felt an unpleasant tingling in my solar plexus, the sort you get when you have the sense that something very bad is about to happen. The thing was I *recognised* that voice – the new voice that Stavros appeared to be using.

'Accent schmaccent,' said Stavros, with a distinctly home counties twang. 'I could never remember my Greek accents anyway.'

'Hang on a second,' said the Dr. 'Your voice has changed. Why are you talking like that?'

'I shall talk as I please. Indeed,' Stavros added, leaning back in his motorised chair, 'I shall talk *like what* I please.'

Linn, standing beside me, sucked in a deep breath.

'Deliberate grammatical solecism, eh?' said the Dr. 'You don't scare me with your heavy-handed mangling of the proper rules of communication.'

'Don't I?'

'Quick, Doctor,' said Linn, grabbing his coat. 'Let's make a run for it. Into the TARDY! Let's get away whilst we still can.'

'I've got to put an end to the beginning of the Garleks first,' said the Dr, looking confusedly about him. 'Let me just —'

He pressed his thumb against the on-switch of the Moronic Screwdriver. A beam of concentrated mor-onification shot out. The molecules of air between the Dr and Stavros became too moronic to continue their Brownian motion and started to freeze out as crystals of ice.

'Too late for that, Doctor, I'm afraid,' declared Stavros. 'Your screwdriver won't avail you.'

There was a loud cracking noise, like a large plank of wood being snapped in half. The Moronic Screwdriver flew from the Dr's hands.

'This is not the end of the Garleks,' declared Stavros. 'It is not the *beginning* of the end of the Garleks. It is not even the end of the beginning of the Garleks. It is, however, the end of *you* Doctor —'

'What?' asked the Dr, slightly non-specifically, con-sidering the circumstances. 'Who . . . do what? *What*?'

Stavros seemed to freeze. There was an atmosphere of indelible menace in the air. Which, of course, is where you'd expect to find atmosphere.

For a moment we all held our breaths.

'He's gone quiet,' the Dr observed, cautiously. 'And motionless.'

'Didn't it strike you as odd that he didn't immediately call for Garlek guards to come defend him?' Linn said, urgently. 'He could have done that with a single finger on his control panel. And yet he did not. I'll tell you what I think: he's *not* what he seems . . .'

'This is *rather* peculiar,' agreed the Dr. 'Extremely. Odd, very.'

And just as he said that, things got a whole lot odder.

Yes. I know that the comma is out of place in that last sentence.

Allow me to explain.

Chapter Eleven

'MEET *ME* — ET!

A crack appeared in the frontal carapace of Stavros's chair. It opened just a hemi-demi-inch, and ran all the way up the front of Stavros's body. Light spilled from the crevice. And then it widened, and two halves swung apart from one another on some unobvious hinge.

'What is going,' started the Dr, and put his mouth into a circle to conclude his sentence *on?* when he was interrupted with a loud *bang*! A metallic stair unfolded from inside Stavros's torso and clanged onto the ground.

'It's a TARDY!' I exclaimed.

'You don't say,' said Linn, with, I feel, uncalled-for sarcasm. 'Did you just figure that out?'

'Oh don't be like *that*,' I said. 'I'm a simple Prose Taylor from Earth. I'm not a fancy Time Gentleman apprentice, like . . .'

'Shh,' said the Dr. 'Somebody's coming out.'

There was the sound of footsteps coming down what appeared to be an immense stretch of staircase. They came closer and closer, clattering of boots on metal steps. The approach took a whole minute; two. Finally, with a little sigh as of exhaustion, a small green figure stepped briskly down to the last few steps and stood on the ground before us all. He, she or it was no more than a metre high. It (let's say) had the face of a rapturous tortoise; but was dressed in a pale green onepiece of faintly military appearance and was wearing big clumpy boots on its small stumpy legs, giving its lower regions a pronounced stumpyclumpy appearance.

'Hiya,' it said. Its voice was squeaky, like a squeegee being wiped across a clean window, or a creaky door being opened slowly. Or like Richard Leaky, whom (if you've ever heard him you'll know) was possessed of a high pitched voice.

'And who in the name of J Jurms and his Po,' asked the Dr, 'are *you*?'

'I'm the ET.' The creature standing before us did a little bow. With a fluid motion its small arm flipped to its side and came back up again holding a boomerang-shaped weapon.

The Dr blanched. Blancmanged. Blancversed. I mean he went white. In the face. And maybe elsewhere about his body too. But I could only see his face.

'That's,' he said, pointing. 'That's— a —'

'It's no blinking Moronic Screwdriver,' said the new-comer, happily.

'It's a TGV!'

'So it is.'

'But those weapons are *outlawed* by the convention of linearity!'

'They *are* outlawed,' agreed the ET. 'Despised and condemned by all civilised people in the Galaxy. And why? Because they are *deadly* to Time Gentlemen! The *only* weapon that bypasses your infuriating ability to *re-un-degenerate yourselves* at the moment of death!'

'Would you please explain what's going on,' said the

Dr, gathering himself and trying for dignity.

'It's perfectly simple,' said the ET. 'I am your nemesis. Your arch enemy.'

'Don't be silly,' said the Dr. 'My arch enemy is called the Master.'

'Tall feller?' said the ET. 'Little triangular-shaped beard? Booming voice? That was me.'

'You?'

'Well, it was my TARDY. You don't need to look so surprised. If your TARDY can take the shape of a Garlek, why mightn't mine take the shape of a tall bearded man with a booming voice?'

'But if you own a TARDY that must mean,' said Linn, 'that you're a ... Time Gentleman?'

'Naturally,' said the ET. 'I'm on my seventieth re-un-degeneration. I seem to have been getting smaller with each of them in turn, actually, for the last dozen or so. Smaller and greener.' He shrugged. 'But what can you do!'

'Seventy?' objected Linn. 'Impossible! Time Gentlemen only re-un-degenerate thirteen times!'

'Usually that is true,' said the ET. 'But I found a way to bypass that little difficulty. It's a long story, and one I'm not inclined to go into right now. I haven't got time anyway. I'm most dreadfully sorry, my dear Doctor, but I'm going to have to kill you.'

'I beg your pardon ...' said the Dr. 'Did you say *kill* me?'

'That's about the long and short of it.'

'But *why*?'

'You're surprised?' said the ET, perhaps disingenuously. 'And yet you were readying yourself to moronify poor old Stavros – when you thought it really was Stavros. I might ask the same thing there. Why?'

'To prevent a worse evil,' said the Dr. 'Incidentally, where is Stavros? The real Stavros?'

'Somewhere hereabouts,' said the ET, gesturing with his weapon vaguely. 'I don't know. All I know is that my TARDY is set to "most evil person on planet" mode.'

'You were about to explain,' said Linn, 'why you feel obliged to murder the Doctor here?'

'To prevent a worse evil,' said the ET, suavely. 'What other justification for murder carries any weight? It's *Linn*, isn't it?'

'You know me?'

'Of course I do! You're training to become a Time Lady, I believe. And you,' turning to me, 'must be Prose? The assistant?'

I gulped by way of answer.

'Ms Trout,' said the ET. 'How would you feel if you were to learn that the whole rationale of the Time Gentlemen – everything they stand for – is profoundly wrong? That tidying up the time lines will lead inevitably to the end of the universe?'

'Don't be silly,' she said at once. 'That's entirely backwards. Without the Time Gentlemen patrolling the timeways, anarchy would ensue. Chaos! That would lead to the end of the universe—'

'I'm afraid it's so,' said the ET, gaily. 'I must murder the Doctor to save the universe.'

'You're a liar!' I exclaimed. Perhaps unwisely.

'Do you say so, Prose Tailor?' he said, smiling wide

enough to display a line of top teeth like the perforated edge of a stamp. 'But I'm not the one with lying and betrayal on my conscience.'

'Oh,' I said, as everything fell into place. 'You tricked me! You wheedled the information out of me – that the Doctor would be sent here, to the time just before the Garleks were sent out into the cosmos; and you arranged to be here *to meet him*! You got here first and lay in ambush for him, disguised as Stavros!'

'Something like that,' said the ET, airily. 'But I've an important question for you, young Prose. Do you know how the cosmos *used* to be?'

'I don't know what you're talking about.'

'What you need to understand about the Time Gentlemen,' said the little green figure, fluently, 'is that their notion of temporary neatness, of the grammar of time – involves a *linear* mindset. They are comfortable with Monday being followed by Tuesday being followed by Wednesday. They are not comfortable with Monday, Tuesday and Wednesday all happening at once.'

'But of course!' cried the Dr. 'How else could it be?'

'I even used to think like that myself,' said the ET. 'When I was a working Time Gentleman I spent decades of my life zipping up and down through time sorting things out, neatening events, eliminating superfluous temporal apostrophes and adding necessary temporal semicolons. Until I saw the error of my ways.'

'There's no error,' said the Dr.

'But there is. Because it's the natural order of the cosmos for Monday, Tuesday and Wednesday *all to happen at once*. Just as it is the natural order for a garden to become overgrown with all manner of weeds – weeds *and* flowers. Or, perhaps a better example might be: just as it is the natural order for language to sprawl beyond rules and grammars, despite the work of all the pedants in pedagogy. To sprawl beyond all rules and grammars and still be effective at communication!'

'I happen,' said the Dr, a little stiffly, 'to like a well-weeded garden. And I happen to think that a grammatically and syntactically correct sentence is aesthetically pleasing.'

'Neater,' said the ET, nodding. 'But neatness isn't the only aesthetic. Prose, let me tell you something. On your homeworld there was a thing called the Fermi paradox. Heard of it?'

'Ah!' I said. 'The *Fermi* paradox! The Fermi *paradox*! No, never heard of that.'

'Well,' said the ET. 'It's about the lack of extra-terrestrial civilisation. Given the size of the universe there ought to be billions of kinds of alien life co-existing; and yet there's no evidence of any. Well, you've had experiences few of your fellows have had. You've seen *some* aliens.'

'Of course,' I said.

'Some. Yet there *should* be billions.'

'I don't understand where you're going with this,' I confessed.

'Only to explain the Fermi paradox. It's the Time Gentlemen, you see. They're the answer. They can't abide a teeming multitude of simultaneous galactic civilisations. They've weeded most of them out. They've all the time in the cosmos, after all. All the time they need to institute hundreds of thousands of varieties of this plan here. This plan – to eliminate the Garleks. That'll be one less alien group cluttering up the place.'

'But the Garleks are the most evil beings in the galaxy!' the Dr objected.

'Nonsense. They make war, it's true. They're cruel. But do you know how many alien races would be left if you eliminated *all* those that made war, or *all* those who were sometimes cruel? None, that's how many. And that's where the Time Gentlemen plan is heading.'

'That's a grotesque pastiche,' said an infuriated Linn, 'a distorting parody of the philosophy of ...'

'And you've no time for parody,' interrupted the ET, scornfully. 'I *know*. Let me put it this way, young Prose. When you were growing up on Earth, my young tike, did you have any knowledge of the Cydermen?'

'No,' I said. 'Not when I was growing up. I met them later, with the Doctor.'

'That's right. You did. You met them because you were in the extratemporal bubble of the Doctor's TARDY. But you'd never heard of them before, when you were growing up on Earth in the twenty-third century?'

'No.'

'Despite the fact that the Cydermen invaded earth in twenty-ten?'

'Did they?' I said. 'I don't remember learning that in history.'

'It's been edited *out* of history. Too messy. The whole Cydermen race – gone. They exist now only as a faint echo in the species subconscious, echoing vaguely in the bizarre fictions of writers and filmmakers. There are whole *groups* of alien races – gone the same way. For instance: did you know that Octopoid Martians invaded Earth in eighteen-eighty-nine, until a zealous Time Gentleman went back to a much earlier Mars and left a fridge door open, depriving the Martian national grid of electricity and causing (domino clacking onto domino) the downfall and death of the whole civilisation. Time Gentlemen? That's— what— they— *do.*'

'By our actions Earth was spared a violent invasion ...' pointed out the Dr.

'And the Martians were spared the bother of living in the first place. Just to make the cosmos *neater.*' He scowled. 'Do you know where it'll lead? To the weeding out of all co-existing races. Eventually the Time Gentlemen will permit to exist only a succession of linearly consequent civilisations – one after the other – like Monday, Tuesday, Wednesday.'

There was an awkward silence.

'Is this true?' I asked the Dr and Linn.

'True? To be sure it is,' said the ET. 'How many alien civilisations were known to your homeworld when you were growing up, Prose?'

'Well, the three of course.'

'So. Imagine this: one day, if the Time Gs have their way, a boy or a girl will be born on Earth and look up at the sky – and it'll be *wholly bare of life*! All the teeming multitudes cross-pollinating one another's civilisations in messy profusion – gone! Nothing at all, except humans pondering an unsolvable Fermi paradox.'

'There are good reasons,' said the Dr, slowly, 'why

the proper order and sequence of the life-forms of the . . .'

'But there's more,' interrupted the ET. 'If it were only that, I'd have qualms about committing – as Ms Trout so accurately says – murder. But there's more than that.'

'What?'

'The very nature of the universe itself. Have you ever wondered,' the ET said, as if what he were saying followed logically from his previous speeches, 'why every hydrogen atom in the universe possesses exactly the same dimensions?'

I looked at Linn. She looked at the Dr. The Dr looked at Linn. I looked at the Dr. Linn and the Dr looked at me. We all three looked at the ET.

'No,' I said eventually. 'I can honestly and without fear of contradiction say, that this is not something I have ever wondered.'

'It's a puzzle, though, ain't it?' said the ET.

'Is it?'

'Oh yes. Very much a puzzle. Puzzly, that's what it is.'

'I'm afraid I've lost the thread a little . . .'

'Hydrogen is the simplest atom. All the other atoms, carbon and beryllium and gallagherlium and so on, they're just variants of hydrogen mashed out by deep gravity wells and high temperature. Inside stars mostly. But what of the *original* hydrogen? Trillions upon trillions, trillions to the power of trillions of hydrogen atoms and every one *exactly the same as all the others*? It's hard to believe, don't you think?'

'You're imagining,' Linn offered, 'a universe in which

some hydrogen atoms were atom-sized and some were the size of a semi-detached house?'

'Not that,' said the ET. 'But, you know. In almost every other manifestation the universe admits of small variations. Microbes are all very small, but not every microbe is precisely the same size. Stars, planets, all differ. Even the speed of light differs depending on whether it passes near a strong gravitational field or not. All these things are different, yet every single atom of hydrogen is exactly the same size? Surely not.'

'I just don't see what you're getting at,' I admitted, as candidly as I could. 'I mean, isn't that just the way hydrogen atoms are?'

'Could somebody just explain to me how we went from the Fermi Paradox to hydrogen atoms?' put in Linn. 'I just can't seem to see the link.'

'Bear with me,' said the ET. 'I'm getting round to it.'

'What is the Fermi paradox anyway?' I asked.

'It's the "For *me?* paradox",' Linn corrected me. 'It's called that because the observer looks around and can't quite believe that the whole cosmos is just there for his individual benefit.'

'You're both wrong,' said the Dr. 'It's the Vermin Paradox – the cosmos ought to be swarming with vermin. But the Time Gentlemen have been carefully pruning and husbanding the cosmos to keep it clean.'

'What was it about hydrogen atoms?' I asked.

'I'll tell you why they're all exactly the same size,' said ET, sighting along the barrel of his curiously shaped weapon. 'Because they're the same atom.'

'The same atom?'

'The same atom.'

'How can they be the same atom? That's absurd. There are many trillions of them all.'

'How can there even be *one* atom?' said ET. 'That's the real question. But there was. One atom of hydrogen. It existed . . .it was the only thing that existed. It lasted through the billions upon billions of years of the cosmos. When it reached the end of time it got bounced back upon itself, lasting counterclockwise through time to the beginning. Then there were two. Then four. Then eight – all the same atom, bouncing back and forth through time. But, you see, that gives the wrong impression – because these replications did not happen *one after the other* in the way I'm describing here, they appeared to the external observer to happen *simultaneously*. This one atom, duplicated trillions of times, suddenly exploded outwards – the Big Bang. Our cosmos.'

'Right,' I said. 'And this is relevant because . . .?'

'Because if the Time Gentlemen get their way then that simultaneity, that messy simultaneity, will be unpicked. That's the inevitable endpoint of the TG philosophy. If you purge the cosmos of all ungrammatical and unsyntactic logic, then eventually you purge it of life. Because life *is mess* – life is the refusal to abide by the rules, the refusal to be constrained by restrictions. Life is evolution – and evolution is the production of parodies of previously existing forms of life! Parody is the process of growth and change! Those who take a zero tolerance approach to parody are enemies of the endless shuffling and recombination, the sometimes beautiful and sometimes alarming mutations that power existence itself.

I used to be a Time Gentleman myself, policing the timeways. But then I realised: the TGs are not the answer to the problem. They *are* the problem.'

'Well,' said the Dr, slightly sneeringly. 'A very pretty speech.'

'Enough Doctor,' said the ET. 'I apologise for having to do this. Murder is never a nice thing. But perhaps you can believe that it is in the service of a higher good. If I let you live you'll destroy the Garleks forever – and then you'll go on to do much worse.'

'I'm sorry!' I burst out. 'It's my fault! I betrayed you, Doctor!'

There was an awkward silence. Linn and the Dr both looked at me.

'I didn't realise he was planning to ... you know, *kill* you,' I said, in an agony of remorse. 'I just thought he was going to ... I don't know.'

'What?' snapped the Dr. 'What did you think he was going to do?'

'I don't know,' I wailed. 'But you killed the only woman I ever loved!'

'What are you talking about?' the Dr snapped. 'That woman in the helmet? You're bonkers. I'm a Time Gentleman! Don't you think that, once we'd sorted out these evil Garleks, I was planning to go back to the moment just before that lady was trapped inside the helmet and rescue her?'

'You,' I gulped, tears in my eyes, 'you *were*?'

'Of course I was! What do you think I am – heartless? It's one of the perks of being a Time Gentleman. One of the few, I might add. You get to go back and undo your mistakes. Pop back in the TARDY, try again 'til I get it right.'

'So that,' I said, realisation dawning, 'was why you were so blasé about her being dead?'

'Nothing ever really dies,' the Dr said. 'Not if you're a Time Gentleman.'

Hope flared in my breast. 'So we can go and get her?'

'Of course.'

'Can we go back now this minute?'

'Well, absolutely, yes,' said the Dr, scratching his chin, 'Just as soon as I get these two trivial things out of the way. Firstly the elimination of the threat posed by the most evil race of beings the galaxy has ever known. And secondly, secondly, something else, slipped my mind, what is it, oh yes, my imminent and painful *death*, you *berk*.'

I turned to the ET. 'Please!' I begged him. 'Please don't murder the Doctor! I'm very sorry I betrayed him to you – but if you let him live he can undo some of the damage he has done. I'm sure he's learned his lesson. You were once a Time Gentleman yourself, you say? You reformed your ways ... why can't you believe he can do the same?'

'Why can't I?' said the ET. 'Well, because I've lived in the future. I know how this story ends. It doesn't end the same way every time, of course; but in every version I've seen the Doctor can't be allowed to live.'

'Please!' I implored. 'We're talking about my only true love! I lost her once – now I discover I can get her back. Don't take her away from me one more time!'

'You need to consider the bigger picture,' advised the

ET. 'Did you ever wonder what the initials d and r stood for?'

'Well,' I said. 'Doctor, obviously.'

The ET shook his lump-shaped green head. 'Not that. *Dictator*. And whilst murder may be a crime, tyrannicide is *not*.'

'Dictator,' I said. 'Really? Is this true, Doctor? Linn?'

'Well, yes,' the Dr admitted. 'But it's not as bad as it sounds. A dictator is simply somebody who dictates – who tells you the correct way of doing something. That's all we do, we Time Gents. We just point out where people have gone wrong ...'

'I think we've been talking long enough,' said the ET. 'Is everybody up to speed now? Does everybody understand what's at stake? If the Doctor here lives he'll eliminate the Garleks, bring your woman back to life, and then go on to cleanse the galaxy of *all mess*. If I execute him, then I'm afraid your woman stays dead. Sorry about that. But otherwise life can continue in its messy and glorious profusion, and the Fermi paradox need never bother us.'

'Go on,' said the Dictator, with sudden bravado. 'Do your worst. Shoot me with your nasty gun! See if I care! You're only going to hit my knee at the height you're pointing it anyway.'

With an agility that one would not automatically associate with his stumpy little legs the ET leapt up and landed on the tray of his Stavros-shaped TARDY. This brought him up to a level where a shot from his death-dealer would shatter the Dr's chest and stop his brain.

'Ah,' said the Dr, in a much less bravado-y voice. 'I see. So it's my brain, is it?'

'That's the fatal zone,' said the ET.

The Dr put his hands up in the air. 'Does this help?' he asked.

'Help?'

'Help you not shoot, I mean? Look, I surrender.'

'It's no good, I'm afraid. This is goodbye, Dictator. No longer shall your kind oppress the Galaxy with your terrible grammatical correctitude—'

'—ness,' corrected the Dr, in a small voice.

'Enough,' said the ET in a sorrowful voice.

I could not believe what was happening in front of my very eyes. 'No,' I cried. 'Wait!'

The ET pressed the muzzle of his weapon close up against the Dr's chest, so as to be quite sure that there was no chance of the shot going wide. I had a ghastly sensation of *déjà vu*. There had to be some way of preventing this event.

The ET pulled his trigger and the deadly weapon discharged. Its explosive bolt of time-energy crashed into the Dr's torso, and he lurched backwards.

He fell.

He crashed to the ground amongst the rubbish of Stavros's lab.

'Ta ta now,' said the ET, hopping back onto the floor. He pressed a button on the outside of his TARDY; the door opened and he scurried inside. A moment later the form of seated Stavros, whiskers and all, shimmered out of vision and disappeared.

This broke whatever spell of inaction had been cast

upon Linn and myself. We rushed over to the dead form of the Dr.

'Doctor!' I cried. It was a cry of despair.

*

'Linn,' I urged. 'You must do something! Take the TARDY, go back in time, undo this terrible thing.'

'I can't,' she said, her voice full of sorrow.

'Don't be like that ...'

'No, I mean I can't. I *really can't*. I don't know how. I've got years of training before me. I'm not a Time Lady, I'm just an apprentice.'

These were very discouraging words indeed. If Linn couldn't operate the TARDY then the Dr was indeed dead, irrevocably. Moreover, Linn and I were both trapped there: stuck on the planet Skary, in the heart of the bunker of a criminally insane fascist Greek chef just at the moment he turned his planet over to the rule of the Garleks. Things looked bleak indeed.

'Bother,' I said.

Then something happened that I was not expecting. The Dr sat up and said two things that sounded, to my jangled ears, rather like non sequiturs. Which is to say, sounded unlike garden pruning scissors. He said, 'has he gone?' And then he said. 'Quick, help me off with my *tie* ...'

'Tie?' I stammered. 'What?'

'Quick!' he urged. 'Quick— quick—' He was scrabbling at his neck. 'I had to wait until I was sure he was gone,' he explained, as he yanked the tie to loosen it. 'Or else I ... there!' The tie was loose, a snake of cloth that wriggled as the Dr flung it through the air. Then in mid-air something strange happened. The tie seemed to explode. It kinked and shreds and bits of fluff flew out from it.

'What ...?'

An instant later a bullet caromed into the far wall. The tie, in two pieces now, fell slowly to the floor.

'My TARDY tie,' the Dr explained, getting to his feet and dusting himself off. 'You know that space between the front and back bit of a tie? That little flat cavity?'

'I have never worn a tie,' I said, honestly enough, but feeling the oddity of my statement.

'Well a tie is actually a sort of tube of cloth,' the Dr was saying. 'Think of a tapering tube pressed flat ... there's your tie. And since this was a TARDY tie, with the logo on it and everything, of course it was considerably bigger inside than it is outside. I've never actually measured it, but I have reason to believe it's about a mile across from front to back.'

'So when the ET shot you ...?'

'The bullet passed into my tie: it was hurtling across the cavity as I lay there. But I had to wait until the ET left, or he'd just shoot me again. It's like towel – you remember that TARDY towel you used to dry yourself off after your dip in the North Atlantic? That was similar technology. The spaces between the strands of towelling were much much *much* larger than the towel itself. That was why it was so extraordinarily good at soaking up water.'

'So that explains the towels,' I said.

Not much of a sentence, really. Considering that I'm a prose tailor, and everything.

'Right!' said the Dr with enormous vigour. 'Let's get on with this averting of terrible consequences, shall we? Put an end to the Garleks – nip back in time to rescue your ladylove – and get away!'

EPILOGUE

My relationship with Lexanco didn't last, of course. The time I spent upon Tapov had its moments, but the main thing I learned there was that I couldn't dance very well. Well, the two things I learned there were, (a) that I couldn't dance very well, and (b) it's hard to keep a woman interested in you if you are flabby and pale and badly co-ordinated when that same woman is surrounded by a whole planetful of lithe, muscular, handsome, graceful and co-ordinated males.

Ah well.

But that's not what I want to talk about in this epilogue.

You've now read my story, tailored out of my own prose, about my experiences with the Dr. If you've read it with any attention you will have spotted a variety of errors of punctuation, and the occasional grammatical solecism. If you've paid even closer attention you *may* have noticed that the story was not arranged according to the rules of sequential and chronologically-linear development. Everything that the Time Gentlemen represent.

This was done on purpose.

You see, I met up with the ET again. I couldn't stop thinking about his words, to be honest; and when I met him again he was able to convince me.

To convince me that the Time Gentlemanly obsession with rules, order and sequence is not only wrongheaded, but actively dangerous to the cosmos.

To convince me to join him in his campaign to save the universe from the Time Gentlemen.

And if you've been able to follow the story this far – if you've survived this dislocation of narrative – then I hope you'll understand. Understand, and maybe join us too . . .

SPECIAL OFFER! SPECIAL OFFER! SPECIAL OFFER!

Your very own MORONIC SCREWDRIVER®!

Only available from Whom Industries plc.[1] Yours for only £399.99 plus postage and packing, placing, platterning and patrolling. And pirouetteing. [Whom plc guarantees that our staff will pirouette at least three times for every order received].

- Bothered by screws?
- Troubled by bolts?
- Tenderised by a meat-tenderiser?
- Worried by global warming?
- Anxiously uncertain about the English translation of the German *angst*?

The answer to all your problems is a MORONIC SCREWDRIVER©!

That's right, a MORONIC SCREWDRIVER ♣ of your very own! Be king of screws with this *handy* device.[2]

> **A professor writes:** 'the usual principle of unscrewing a screw is that a screwdriver must be aligned and inserted in perfect connection with the screw head, and then rotated under pressure *not once but many times*. This is excessively tiresome, especially to those galactic species whose forearms and wrists are not fitted with the capacity for uninhibited rotation. What is needed is a screwdriver that operates according to a radically new principle. Either that, or somebody else to do the screwdriving instead of me whilst I have a little sit down and a cup of tea.'

The MORONIC SCREWDRIVERO™ operates according to a radically new principle. Simply point your MORONIC SCREWDRIVER⊕ at the screw, engage the patented MORONICIZER RAY with your thumb, and watch as the screw goes all moronic, probably falling out of its own stupid accord, the stupid twit, hah! Any screw to which the patented MORONICIZER RAY is applied will become too *idiotic*, *brainhurty* and *durr!* to be able to continue doing its screw-ish work of holding stuff together.

Wam! Bam! Thank you Whom!

[WARNING: do not use this device to grout wax out of your ear. Should you accidentally activate the MORONIC SCREWDRIVER hellomum! **inside your skull, Whom plc can take no responsibility for the moronification that may result.]**

---

1 Parodically Limited Company
2 PLEASE NOTE: Device fits most hands. If your hand is unusually large, small, or tentacular, please refer to manufacturers' handbook/tentaclebook

THE MONSTERS OF DR WHOM

The complete range of monsters against which the Dr and his apprentice have battled is now available via Monsieur Monster, the specialist Monster Introduction Agency

THE GARLEKS
Available in clove, megaclove, supermegaclove, hyper-supermegaclove and Big.

THE CYDERMEN
♪♫ *"Oi am a zyder thinker, oi think it all of the day ..."* ♪♫

THE SLUTTYTEENS
'Sluttyteen' over-skin suits now available in Matt Lucas or Nicholas Soames sizes.

THE SKI DEVILS
Rising from the depths of water (well, of frozen water on the slopes of the Alps, but that's still technically water) to terrify innocent skiers ...

THE SONTAGANS
A fearsome sect of fanatics whose life is dedicated to the writing of Susan Sontag.

Dr WHOM
PAYS, TRIBUTE
TO Dr WHO

Who could forget the roll of acting honour, the range of genius that embodied Dr Who for generations of eager viewers?[3] Deathless their names shall be; never shall their glory fade; they shall not grow old as we who lack the capacity to regenerate our bodies via some frankly implausible cod-biological strategy shall grow old. Let us list them here, names as familiar to us as the names of our own families, in an if-you-will roll of Who-honour. Whonour, indeed:

Patrick Hartwell. Hartnell. Hatywell. Or was it William? Hmm. Not that it matters: nobody can remember him these days anyway.

Patrick Troughton. He was short. He wore a natty black jacket, black moleskin trousers. He had black hair, black eyes. In fact, as I recall him to memory, he had grey skin.

---

3 The first 'Who' in this sentence does not refer to 'Dr Who' obviously. If it did, then the sentence would be saying that *Dr Who* could forget the actors who played Dr Who, which would be a strange thing to say. Although, now that I come to think of it, there may be something in that ... as if to say, the archetype that is Dr Who need have no cognizance of the individual actors who have embodied him over the decades ... but, no, on second thoughts, that would just be silly.

That can't be a good sign, can it? Medically I mean? Let me put it this way: if *I* woke up one morning and looked in the shaving mirror and saw that my skin had gone literally *grey*, I'd get down to the GP pretty sharpish, let me tell you. 'Here!' I would say. 'What are you going to do about this? My entire dermis as grey as gunmetal, and my eyes, previously a rather fetching blue, gone all black. I want to know what you're going to *do* about it, that's what I want to know. And *don't* try giving me some brush-off prescription for a "special medicated cream" that we all know is just plain moisturiser, that's not going to *fly* with me, sonny. I want specialists from all over the world congregating to discuss this astonishing dermatological development, from off-pink to grey in one night. I want high-tech treatments.'

Anyway, the *point* here, the point, is that nobody can really remember Troughton either.

Jon Pertwee. Sean Pertwee's dad, you know. Curly white hair, red velvet jacket, no 'h' in his first name. That's what was memorable about him. Obviously most people called 'John' are happy enough to carry the h. But not 'Jon' Pertwee. I mean, what's that supposed to prove, anyway? That's some strange affectation, right there: like he's saying 'oh, oh, I can afford to buy this crushed velvet jacket and to drive about in a *personal hovercraft* but I can't afford the h for the middle of my first name'. Is that what he's saying? Because, *let me tell you*, personal hovercrafts are both extremely expensive and frankly unnecessary. If he can afford that, he can sure as dammit afford the 'h'. Why can't he drive a Cortina, like everybody else? Or else that other Ford car, the one with the three gears and the single windscreen wiper, the one with the SFy-name, what was it called? I find that kind of behaviour despicable. Like those aristocrats who go around in really tatty tweed trousers with saggy crotches and holes in the knee, 'Oh look at me, I'm rich enough to put all my children through Eton but I'm too poor to buy new trousers.' It makes me sick, I don't mind telling you. It makes me actually nauseous with fury. I may have to go and have a little lie down, right now.

Tom Baker. *Now* we're talking! This is the real Dr Whom material. Big booming voice. Scarf. Getting off with one of his beautiful assistants in real life. *That's* what we're looking for. And now he's doing *Little Britain* voice-overs. Am I the only one to think that this is something of a come down, really?

Peter Davidson. The problem I have (I'll be frank) with this sort of name is that it slips about in one's memory. Don't you think? Is it Peter *David*son, or David *Peter*son? Either is as good as the other, frankly. A name should have more fixity, more memorability, or what's the point of it? Jack Johnson, John Jackson, Russell David, David Russell, who could ever tell them all apart? No. Either you want completely *non*-interchangeable fore-name-surname combos, something like Jim Czccrych, or Alexander p, or else you want to short-circuit the whole process by calling yourself Robert Robertson, or something. There's a small sort of genius in the latter strategy, of course. And, now that I'm on the subject, *why* was Robert Robertson *never asked* to play Dr Who? He'd have been *brilliant*. 'Ahhhh, now that the Daleks are defeated, I can promise the peoples of the Earth their continued survival and prosperity, and— *this* round of applause.' You see what I mean?

The guy who came after Peter Davidson. Curly hair. Don't recall the name. He doesn't seem to have the curly hair any more, judging by his appearances on TV nowadays reminiscing about his days playing the Doctor. But that's no crime. Baldness is not a crime. Arson, *that's* a crime; not baldness.

The guy who came after *the guy who came after Peter Davidson*. Don't recall his name either. I've got 'Baker' buzzing around in my head, but that might just be because Tom Baker made such a deep impression in the role. Sylvester Baker, was it? Incidentally, and whilst we're on the subject of Tom Baker, I've a question: do you think that Tom Baker ever went up to his own mother and sang the Boney-M hit single 'Ma Baker' when that hit the charts in the mid-1970s? *M-m-m-m-ma, Ma Baker, she carried a gun* – because if it had been *me*, I *definitely* would have done. That would have been *hilarious*. Of course, since my mother is called Roberts, and since there's no song 'Ma Roberts', I've never had the chance.

Paul McGann. Given that there are about four hundred McGann brothers, all of whom work in TV, and all of whom look exactly alike, I'm rather proud of myself for being able to remember the one who played the Dr for that crappy Americanised one-off TV-film. But since he can't even be bothered to turn up on TV nowadays to reminisce about his days playing the Doctor I think we should throw the tarpaulin of historical forgetfulness over him, nail it down at the edges, and neither mention nor even think about him ever again.

Christopher Eccleston. Oh, everybody loves Christopher Eccleston. They love him as a serious actor, and they *loved* him as Doctor Who. How could they not? He completely abandoned the fey, curly-headed, southern English weirdness and instead played the character as an out-of-work northern builder on e. Leather jacket. Big *chunky* leather jacket, and a nose apparently borrowed from a much *much* larger face. That's Eccleston.

I mean, I know he's a highly respected actor and everything, but he has 'Eccles' in his surname. It's the *main part* of his surname, for crying out glaven. How can anybody take him seriously? Would you take *me* seriously if I were called 'Adam Doughnutton'? NO, you would NOT.

Casanova guy. I can't *tell* you how much my wife wishes to enjoy carnal relations with the actor playing the new Doctor Who. I can't tell you because my eyes mist up with furious despair at the very thought. Curse him. Curse his perfectly shaped features and his trim body. Curse him to all bejiminey.

Who will follow in these illustrious footsteps? The

Doctor has only twelve regenerations, after all, so there can be only thirteen actors given this ultimate honour. Or else he has *thirteen* regenerations, so there can be only *twelve* actors who – no, that can't be right. So: the team here at Dr Whom offer up our suggestions as to whom (ahem!) might be waiting in the wings to take on this esteemed role.

Doctor Who 11: *Tom Hanks*. He would be a *brilliant* choice. He could even change his name to 'Tom "Dr" Whanks'. Which is something I suggest he do because it is a cross between 'Who' and 'Hanks' and for no other reason. What I mean is, I'm suggesting Hanks should play the part because he's a very versatile actor, and is a big star to boot. He could pull off the Dr, don't you think? He could easily pull him off. Easily slip into that role.

Doctor Who 12: *Boris Johnson*. It's the part Boris was born to play. And, can I just add, with respect to what I said a moment ago about Tom Hanks, that I only meant to *compliment* Mr Hanks on his range and technical expertise as an actor. The whole 'whanks' thing . . . obviously, now, I rather wish I hadn't coined that particular portmanteau word. It literally *didn't occur* to me that people might read it as a variant upon 'wanks'. The thought never crossed my mind. It would have been monstrously disrespectful of me to suggest that, should he ever accept the BBC's invitation to play Who, fans or people in general would start calling him 'Dr Whanks'. The thought of that would, I'm sure, act as something of a disincentive. And I'd hate to think that I'd played a part, howsoever small, in disincentivising an actor of Tom's stature from taking up an iconic role like Dr Who.

Doctor Who 13 – Simon Hoggart, star of Radio 4's 'News Quiz' and English comedic eccentric. It's the part Simon was born to play. He could change his name to 'Simon "Dr" Whoggart', which works much *much* better than the whole 'Tom Whanks' thing, which I deeply regret, I really do, I'm most dreadfully sorry I mentioned that now. Sorry I ever brought it up. I really can't apologise enough. Tom? Tom— if you're reading this, *please* believe me when I say that I apologise, wholeheartedly and unreservedly, for morphing your name to 'Whanks', it was in no way 'fair comment' and was not intended to impugn your professional or personal integrity in any way. I hereby undertake never to repeat it. I'm appallingly sorry. I am.